Life by Numbers

ELIZABETH BARBER

Life by Numbers

Copyright Elizabeth Barber © 2017
www.psychicbeth.com

'Universal Number Attraction' system © Elizabeth Barber
www.universalnumberattraction.com

ISBN 978-1-912009-81-7

Published by Compass Publishing UK
www.compass-publishing.com

Designed and typeset by The Book Refinery Ltd

I wish to dedicate this book in memory of my friend Liz,
who always believed in my work.

CONTENTS

About 'Universal Number Attraction'

The *'Universal Number Attraction'* is a powerful and intelligent system which works with the energy and vibration of numbers to deliver meaningful messages. It links people and numbers together in a unique way. This process is where numbers are synchronised and matched to a relevant message specifically aimed at you. This will contain truth, guidance and clarification about your life and its challenges, therefore enabling you to take any appropriate action.

'Universal Number Attraction' is a different concept to numerology, therefore they should not be confused with each other. Unlike numerology, *'Universal Number Attraction'* does not require your birth date or name to present information to you. It's more about asking the Universe for help, assistance and guidance and then being open to receiving the answers through numbers that are put in your path and that grab your attention.

It's a similar concept to Cosmic Ordering where we ask the Universe to deliver and manifest our expectations and desires, but done via a number system, which corresponds with a direct message at a time in your life when you need it most.

I've been working with this concept for many years and have used this powerful tool as a way of being open to messages which have been sent from the Universe. It became apparent to me that numbers were not just about mathematics, telling the time or used to count money. There were also hidden meanings within them and not just in single numbers either, but in number sequences too.

The Universe is intelligent and will deliver the correct number or numbers that will inform, guide and motivate you.

You'll gain insightful information, help with problem solving and a clear vision of how to obtain your goals and desires.

This method is simple, effective and brings astonishing results. All that is required is an open mind and to trust in the power of *'Universal Number Attraction'.*

Introduction

The purpose of this book is to guide and inform you by using *'Universal Number Attraction'*. This is when the Universe sends you signs through numbers to help you with your life and its challenges: to assist, guide and support you, to make changes and to see things from a new perspective.

As a Psychic Medium, Clairvoyant, Reiki Master and Animal Communicator, I've met many people who tell me they're looking for answers to life's problems and dilemmas. Often, they report feeling lost, stuck and confused. They tell me they're seeking helpful guidance; searching for a way to see things more clearly, to have hope for the future and to feel motivated.

Each week, for five years, I was lucky enough to have my own Show on a local radio station *'Psychic Beth's Spiritual Calling Show'* broadcasting every Sunday evening. Often the phone lines were full of listeners desperate to receive a comforting and helpful messages. I realised that I was unable to reach out to all those that needed insightful information and the demand was greater than the supply! This frustrated me and prompted me to tune into my spirit guides to offer a solution. My guides told me of *'Universal Number Attraction'* and gave me the idea for this book. It's a system of using numbers to correspond with a message, at a time when you need it most. A fast and easy way that you can access, and it enables you to receive a guiding message.

In my Spiritual work, I've always been aware that I have Spirit Guides that channel information to me. Often this is about other people and their past, present and even future. My guides showed me that by using numbers which are all around us, messages can be unlocked. Many of these messages are delivered in a straight forward manner, which may feel hard hitting at times, but their aim is to deliver the truth and to engage your thoughts in a fresh and positive way. My guides explained the necessity for this brevity and how important it was not to 'fluff' them out, as they'll have a stronger impact and relevance to your current situation.

I believe numbers carry energy and vibration, therefore can offer insightful information for your future. Numbers have great Spiritual significance and are widely used in Numerology, Tarot and Astrology. As I focussed on each number, my spirit guides could channel information to me, and by using my oracle cards and intuition, I was able to seek the meaning for each number.

Numbers are all around us, we see them everywhere. On clocks, in our diary, registration plates etc. We use them each day, whether it's for timekeeping, making calculations, checking temperatures or to establish scientific results etc. In fact, we use and rely on them so much they're part of our daily routine, therefore we often take them for granted. It's hard to think of an application where you don't use numbers. So, it makes perfect sense that their power and ability can also bring personal, and insightful information.

How to use this book

This book has reached you for a purpose, whether it was a gift, an impulsive purchase, a recommendation or you just happened to come across it, the power of the Universe brought it into your life for a reason.

In order to use this book effectively, it's helpful to understand the concept of 'Universal Number Attraction'. It's just like Cosmic Ordering, where we put our thoughts out to the Universe and await the results. Therefore, we can ask the Universe for a number, or a pattern of numbers to appear in our lives and be shown to us. This will then correspond with a meaningful message relevant to your situation.

This book has been designed for ease of use, so you can access meaningful messages quickly and conveniently. By keeping a copy close to hand, it ensures that when a number pops up in everyday life (especially when you've asked for help) you can quickly read and analyse the meaning.

There's no right or wrong way to use this book and once you become familiar with its concept, you'll soon be using in it in your own unique way. By trusting your own intuition and your gut feelings, this book will become valuable for advice and guidance, not only for yourself but also your friends and family. Keep it with you so you can refer to it when numbers are presented to you. It's also a great icebreaker at parties and good conversation piece. The more you use it, the more numbers will appear - in all kinds of situations - offering you insightful information through a corresponding message.

I feel it's important to mention that you don't have to have any particular beliefs or follow a certain religion to use it, as the Universe works alongside all of us regardless. All that's required to gain effective results, is being open minded enough to give it a go. It can be used for both serious questions, when you have important decisions to make or used in a fun way, when you're with friends.

Some suggestions to get you started:

- Think about a situation that's in your life, something that you would appreciate some advice about. Send that thought out to the Universe. Then be observant as a number will be sent to you in response to your request. It can appear in many ways. When you see the number (or numbers) you will instinctively know that the Universe has delivered, then consult the book. Digest the message and heed the advice.

- Hold the book in your hands whilst thinking of your question or dilemma, then flick to a page of the book and go where guided. You will be drawn to the number that will help.

- Ask the Universe to put a number (or numbers) into your mind, then look it up.

- Write your question down on a piece of paper, carry it with you and look out for the number to appear.

- Think about the question or challenge in your mind, ask the Universe for a number, then just look out for it in the next few hours. (Or, it could just pop up in your thoughts, so use that.)

By being open to signs from the Universe, the numbers will appear.

Common places where numbers appear:

* Your numbers can and will appear in any situation. Here are some typical scenarios where you will see them.

* On clocks, particularly number sequences e.g. 1.11, 1.23, 4.44, 5.55, 6.06 etc.

* Restaurant table numbers.

* Door numbers, especially when visiting somewhere new.

* Car registration plates, often this will be accompanied with your initials or your name, so be watchful when out travelling.

* On billboards and posters.

* By seeing repeated numbers in your daily routine e.g. you keep seeing the same number over and over in a few hours.

* Whilst watching TV or using the internet.

You may get a single number relating to one message, or, several numbers enabling you to access a variety of messages that give you a longer and more detailed reading when put together.

This book is designed for ease of use and you're encouraged to use it in your own unique way.

The Power of the Peacock

I felt very strongly that it was important to use the image of a peacock to illustrate this book.

The peacock is an elegant and colourful bird who represents spirituality, guidance, protection and awakening. The tail feathers have 'eyes' and this is associated with clairvoyance and the ability to see the past, present and future.

In dreams, the peacock's message is to 'show the world who we truly are and that anything is possible'.

The peacock guides us into self-belief and to trust in our own intuition.

The vibrant colours of the peacock also have significance. **Blue** represents communication and is linked to the throat chakra, reminding us to speak our truth and to have the courage to speak out and express ourselves. **Green** represents harmony and healing from every aspect; physically, mentally, emotionally and spiritually. **Gold** signifies wealth, abundance and the ability to manifest into our lives anything we so desire. **Purple** signifies clairvoyant ability, spiritual awareness and is powerful in individuality and creativity. It's also associated with royalty and brings with it great knowledge and wisdom.

The Numbers

1   Stop listening to others and trust your own thoughts and decisions. After going in many different directions, at last the way forward will be clear. Look forward to the month of January to start afresh.

2   Relationships have become strained and difficult, yet there is a way back. Talking and communication is key and being together is important. Take time out together.

3   You're looking to expand and grow. This will bring new elements and new people into your life. This is a good time to start planning and to take action. You may feel as though finances are a problem but you will find that extra cash that you need.

4   This is a time of completion and endings. You are ready to sign contracts and to draw a line under the past. No more moping around. As you finish something in your life, you will feel as though a huge relief has been lifted from your shoulders.

5   You're feeling very tempted. This has placed you into a moral dilemma. You know what the right thing to do is, but temptation is ruling your head. Move forward with caution, as a difficult time may lie ahead.

6 Travel is all around you right now. Go on that journey you've been planning, move abroad or look at job possibilities that reflect this. Great happiness will be yours.

7 You're experiencing feelings of jealousy and anger. Your feelings are valid for a situation you have been facing but nevertheless they are negative and destructive to you. Remember karma is a wonderful thing, so relax, sit back and trust that you will be the onlooker when the balance is redressed.

8 Investments will pay off, but sometimes you need to speculate before you can accumulate. Business decision's or new ventures are favoured right now.

9 Be honest, tell the truth and speak out. Keeping things bottled up is causing you great stress and anxiety. Have a chat with a friend, meditate, relax and gain perspective, as you will find that you have blown things out of proportion.

10 New ideas and a fresh way of thinking is required in this situation. You have received the wrong advice or have listened to those who have not had your best interests at heart. Reconsider your decision.

11 Vehicle problems could be an issue; remember a stitch in time saves nine! By getting work done on your vehicle or those you oversee, will prevent hefty bills in the future.

 12 Stop and think about your actions. Avoid addictive behaviours and stop procrastinating. You are getting stuck in a rut and it's time to get out. Failure to do so will result in you feeling frustrated with a low mood. By adopting a new proactive routine, zest and vitality will be restored.

 13 Take up a new hobby or pastime. Consider going back to something you used to love. Your creativity needs to be unleashed.

 14 Someone in the spirit world is drawing close around you at this sad time. Take strength and comfort as they send their healing out to you. Remember things get better in time.

 15 Due to physical fatigue and mental exhaustion, you're not best placed to make competent decisions. Take time to rest and rejuvenate. Once refreshed then make a choice.

16   A job offer is on the cards. It may not be exactly what you were looking for but it is a great stepping stone to your future.

 17   A chance meeting with an old friend or a new acquaintance will reveal more than you expect. Keep this person close, as they will be a great ally and confidant.

 18   A transitional period lies ahead. Realisation and new beginnings await. The next 4 weeks will require more self-confidence from you. Stand up and be counted.

 19   A new business venture is calling you. Outline a plan of action. Write your ideas down on paper. Discuss with a business advisor or a trustworthy friend. Then look at ways to set things in motion.

 20   Your hard work and persistence is now paying off. Beware not to rest on your laurels though and keep your finger on the pulse. You will soon be set to soar!

21   Indulge yourself in some 'me' time. Spend time in doing what you love. Have a break from work and nurture your soul by walking along the coastline or by a river.

 22   You will soon be embarking on a train journey. Make travel arrangements carefully ensuring that you double-check the details, then enjoy the destination.

 23   Luck is on your side. Competition wins, being recognised for achievements at work and other 'lucky' situations will shine over you. This period is set to last for the next 6 months.

 24   Distant memories from the past are going to be brought into your future. Old flames, friends or relationships will be tracking you down and making contact within the next 6 weeks.

 25   Children or teenagers need support and advice right now. Reach out to them and share your knowledge and compassion.

Your diet is lacking in essential vitamins and minerals. It may be time to get an MOT from your GP and take stock of your dietary intake. Incorporate wholesome foods, fruit and vegetables and where possible eat organic produce to give you more vitality.

Health issues including aches and pains are around you. Look at your posture, especially when driving or travelling in the car. Order a new mattress and get some sensible shoes. This change can make a big difference.

A night out with your friends is called for. Good fun, laughs and giggles and letting your hair down will be excellent therapy for you.

New people will appear into your life during the next 3 months. If you are single this is a great time to meet a new partner. Be prepared by getting a new haircut, new clothes and some exercise. This will give you the confidence boost that's needed to pursue things further.

Stop burying your head in the sand, wake up and smell the coffee! Sort out those financial difficulties that have been worrying you. Make phone calls to resolve these issues, you'll then feel as though the weight has been lifted off your shoulders.

31 New learning is the answer. College courses or home study will give you a better understanding of something you love. This will enhance your career in future months.

 32 This is a time to get in touch with your own psychic gifts and clairvoyance. Read, watch and listen. Your intuition is kicking in. Remember to trust this ability, as it will serve you well in the future.

 33 Property management, house redevelopment and building work is something you're good at. A new challenge is on the way. Grab this opportunity as it will bring financial rewards.

 34 Investments from the past can be fruitful right now. Check any shares, pension, savings accounts and premium bonds etc. Finances are ripe for the picking.

 35 Heart breaking and difficult situations are in your life currently. Remain optimistic about the future as things will change for the better.

36   It's time to take a chance or risk. Come out of your comfort zone and embrace life. Things will change as you alter your perceptions of those around you.

 37   Doing your own research will pay dividends. Read, explore the internet or talk to a professional as this will give you the evidence you need.

 38   New pets or working with animals will be a part of your life very soon.

 39   The time has come to end or retreat from a relationship that has become destructive or unbalanced.

 40   A friend needs your help and support right now. Be there for them and offer a shoulder to cry on.

41 Start a new website or blog page. This will be very beneficial to you in more ways than you could imagine.

 42 A tall gentleman with dark hair and glasses is about to contact you. Listen to his wise words, his advice will invoke huge changes.

 43 Foreign travel or links abroad are very favourable at the moment. Book a holiday or visit friends and family who live on foreign soil. You'll be glad you did.

 44 Spend time with family members closest to you. You have been so busy lately, you've been neglecting them. Quality time is essential.

 45 Music can lift your mood. Feelings of sadness or depression have made you feel suppressed and low. Give yourself a lift by seeing a live band or listening to one of your favourite pop artists.

46 A day out with children or young adults will not only be fun but will give you opportunities to talk and communicate with them effectively.

 47 De-clutter and throw items away. It's time for a spring clean! Take items to the charity shop, car boot sales or sell them on eBay. Think of friends and family that will benefit from some of the things you no longer need, it'll give you a 'feel good boost' and your home will look great. Your mind will clear, giving clarity to your thoughts.

 48 Get out into nature, take some photographs and appreciate what's around you. Use these images to create pictures for the home or cards for friends.

 49 Think long and hard before making this decision as it is life changing. Do not rush or act in haste. Talk to a professional about it first.

 50 Yes – this is the right thing to do. You just need some reassurance from those around you.

51 You are confused. This is because you are not managing your time effectively. Start to plan your day, make rota's and ask for help with tasks. You can't do everything by yourself.

52 No – the time is not right. Reconsider and reflect upon this.

53 Extra finances are needed. Look at how you can raise the extra money you need. Selling old phones, CD's and similar items can really help.

54 Start writing a book or magazine article. Focus on a subject you know a lot about and share your knowledge with the world.

55 To lift your spirits and raise your self-esteem, go shopping! Get some new clothes, shoes and accessories. New colours you don't normally wear will make you feel good. Watch the compliments flow in.

56 Someone around you is not being completely honest and is wearing a mask. Be cautious and keep your ideas to yourself.

 57 Start a new hobby, take dance classes, IT classes or join a club. This will give you a new friend base and more social dates on your calendar.

 58 Dream big, you can achieve your goals far easier than you think. Synchronicity is on your side, watch as your dreams grow.

 59 Holistic therapies are great for your health at the moment. Acupuncture, Indian head massage, Reiki healing, Aromatherapy or Reflexology will be a great way to relax and de-stress.

 60 News of a birth or pregnancy brings great blessings and brings people together.

61 A meeting with a new person shows great potential for a long-term relationship. You'll have lots in common and feel comfortable in their presence.

62 Good news is on the way. Look out for it in the post, by phone or email.

63 Make more of an effort. Stop making excuses to your friends or family. Make more time for them.

64 A newspaper article will give you a great idea that you can turn into a profitable business.

65 Yes, take the opportunity that is offered to you.

66   Join a gym, go on a diet or adapt a healthy lifestyle. More exercise is needed.

67   June 28th, July 2nd, and August 12th will be significant days. Make a note of them on the calendar immediately.

68   Completion dates are drawing close. Check any MOT's for vehicles, renewal of insurances etc. This will ensure you will not miss a deadline for something important.

69   Make special time for a partner. A romantic dinner, a love letter or go on a date. You will be glad you did!

70   A key to a new front door will be in your hands soon.

71 Confide in a trusted friend or talk to your GP or counsellor. Therapy is what is needed for this situation.

 72 You are feeling victimised and sorry for yourself. Take charge of your life. Be authentic and real. Speak your mind and be honest with yourself. What is it that you desire? If something is not working, do something about it.

 73 Your soul mate is on their way to you. Put yourself into social situations in order to meet them. Don't be shy, you're a great person.

 74 By next Christmas you will have manifested great people into your life. Be positive, smile more and believe in yourself.

 75 Make amends, say sorry and put things right. A peace offering is required.

76 Honesty is the best policy. Be very open and wear your heart on your sleeve. Let someone see the real you.

77 Be strong not gullible. Do not be taken in by someone who just tells you what you want to hear.

78 A high maintenance relationship needs getting back on track. Enough is enough. Strike a deal that works for all concerned or move on.

79 Artistic endeavours and creativity can fill you full of awe and wonder. Think outside the box to experience something new. You will surprise yourself by visiting places such as art museums, drawing classes or even a course in photography.

80 Make the most of yourself. Indulge in a face mask, whiten your teeth, shape your eyebrows or even have a fake tan! Enjoy the pampering and watch heads turn.

81 Instead of high street shopping, go on a charity shop day. You will find some unique outfits, fun things for your home and remember to check out the book sections. You can get a lot for your money and you are helping a good cause too.

82 Make some homemade goodies such as cakes, jams and pickles etc. They can be very simple or more complex. These will make great gifts for your friends and you can personalise them with a meaningful message.

83 A new job offer is close. Do not worry, you'll make a great success of it.

84 Drop your guard and let your defences down. If you don't, you'll scare someone away.

85 Romantic liaisons prove to be good fun and you will experience joy and happiness with this person.

86 Someone with the initial 'R' will offer help and support in a difficult situation. Accept this gracefully.

 87 You're feeling bored and stuck in a rut. Book some theatre tickets or go and see a show, it'll give you a well needed lift.

 88 Eat a vegetarian diet for the next few days. Limit any alcohol intake and drink plenty of water. This is a fruitful time to honour your body by going on a healthy detox.

 89 It's a good time to come out of your comfort zone and to push yourself forward. You never know what your limits are until you try.

 90 We all make mistakes and sometimes get things wrong. To recognise this brings wisdom and experience. Do not regret the past, just learn from it.

We all get stabbed in the back from time to time. People can be very cruel and unkind. Don't take revenge, just believe in Karma. Sit back, watch and wait as you'll be having the last laugh.

Make a list of your strengths and weaknesses, be extremely honest. Identifying them will accelerate your own self development. This will increase your spiritual knowledge and how you connect with people.

The best way to lose weight is to eat more healthily and get more exercise. There's no need to go on a crash diet. Eat slowly and eat less. Invest in a dance DVD and bop around your living room, have fun, you'll soon feel a 100 times better.

People in glass houses should not throw stones. Get your own affairs in order before you criticise someone else.

Stop trying to be like everyone else. Focus on being your own authentic self. You're hiding your light under a bushel, now is the time to show the world who you really are.

96 It's time to stop worrying about what others think of you. You are a very sensitive person and you take criticism to heart. Stop absorbing another's negativity, instead allow it to bounce off you and ignore it.

97 It's time to get your skates on as you have been putting things off for far too long. Start immediately.

98 You seem to have lost your mojo! Get motivated, turn over a new leaf to kick a habit and use positive thinking to start afresh. New beginnings are just around the corner.

99 Take on a new challenge and do something good. Organise a charity event or raise money for a worthy cause. It'll raise your self-esteem, push you to your limits and give you the feel-good factor.

100 You've reached a new milestone in your life. Changes and transformation can now follow. New career paths, and new relationships are yours for the taking. Go for it!

To obtain closure on a given situation is healing and helpful. This will resolve an issue that's been troubling you. Either talk to the person whom it concerns, or decide to draw a line under it.

121

Music lifts and reorders your brain signals. When you feel low, put on some of your favourite music and sing along. You'll feel elevated and optimistic.

122

Take a proactive approach where finances are concerned. Your situation can be vastly improved by discussing your money worries with a non-profit making agency such as the Citizen's Advice Bureau.

123

Instead of having sleepless nights about an ongoing problem, consult with a professional. The internet will give you the choices you need.

124

With so many issues around you, it's no wonder you are feeling bogged down, as if the World is against you. To combat this, make a list of these problems and put them in order of importance and priority. Then tackle one at a time and you'll soon realise that things are not as bad as you think.

125

126 A financial windfall is coming to you in the next 3 months. Invest carefully and do not fritter it away as it will be a long time until you get a boost like this again to your bank balance.

127 There is a friend around you right now who needs you. Be selfless and offer a compassionate ear.

128 You are making too many commitments and spreading yourself too thinly. Cut down where you can.

129 Be wary of giving away too much of your time for free. Certain people are draining your energy. This will result in you feeling tired and agitated. Protect yourself from this behaviour.

130 Keep everything in balance. Don't take criticisms too much to heart. Let others' negative attitudes bounce off you and rise above their destructive comments.

131   It's time to take on a new challenge or lifestyle. You are ready and able to do it.

 132   What or who have you been tolerating for too long? You need to address this situation and honour yourself by saying no.

 133   Organisation is lacking in your life right now. Start making lists of important jobs and tasks you need to tackle. Put this list in a place where you can see it and tick things off as you complete them.

 134   Stop getting caught up in other people's drama. This will just cause you to feel upset, drained and exhausted. Instead, focus on activities that are close to your heart.

 135   Do not use your credit card unless you can pay it off at the end of the month. You're getting too tempted by material items you don't really need.

136 Take a step back and breathe. Stop rushing around. You're creating your own stress and anxiety at this time.

 137 Do the right thing and make a complaint or report someone, morally it's the correct course of action.

 138 Give yourself a deadline of completion on a pressing matter. This will stop you from procrastinating and putting it off.

 139 A task is almost at completion, so keep going and don't give up at the last hurdle.

 140 Ask for help, stop pretending everything is okay. People are happy to support you. Do this before things get too much, that way the weight from your shoulders will be lifted quickly.

151 Organise your environment into something that will work for you. Clear out a room, your handbag, or briefcase etc. Your motivation and mojo will then return.

152 When running your own business or if in self-employment, give more than your customers/clients expect. That way, they will recommend you to others. Watch your business grow!

153 Trust your own judgement in making this decision. Don't think about the pro's and cons for too long or you will miss the window of opportunity.

154 It's time to walk away. Deep down you already know that this is the right decision. When something isn't working, let it go.

155 Trust your instinct in this situation and look forwards. Don't be afraid to change your plans as new opportunities arise.

156   If something sounds too good to be true, then it normally is. Proceed with caution.

 157   Don't give up on achieving your mission. Gather more evidence and information in order to move forward with your plans. Success will be yours.

 158   Now is the right time to make commitments or say yes to any proposals, especially where romance is concerned.

 159   No, the time is not right to pursue this idea or project. Wait and gain more information before proceeding.

 160   Make time and be very understanding around children. The changes they're experiencing are making them feel scared and confused. Mixed emotions are hard to deal with. They need your love and support.

171 Eye strain and headaches can be symptomatic of needing an eye test. Book one today.

 172 Be proactive and stand up for what you believe in. Organise a charity dinner or get sponsorship for an event. It will give you more confidence and a sense of achievement.

 173 Doing research and looking into your family background or creating a family tree brings some interesting surprises and revelations. Stories from the past can have a bearing on the future.

 174 To nurture your inner child by letting your hair down and having fun will give you much needed relief during this time of anxiety and stress.

 175 A new work colleague will become a faithful friend. Welcome them with open arms as they enter your life.

176 Sometimes the only person you can trust to make important decisions is yourself. Trust your gut instinct and don't hesitate.

 177 Lady luck is shining down on you. This lucky streak will be with you for the next 3 to 4 weeks, so be sure to take advantage of this fruitful time.

 178 Drawing closer to older family members at this time will be very much welcome, so make the effort.

 179 Having a financial breakdown of your incomings and outgoings will show you exactly where savings can be made. It's time to tighten your belt and save for the future.

 180 Just when we think we have our life back on track something re-emerges from the past. This can feel like a setback, but it's part of your healing process. Tell a friend, in confidence, how you're feeling about this situation. Deal with it and closure will follow.

191 Stop getting upset due to other people's thoughtless comments and actions. Rise above it and don't let them bother you.

192 You need to beat the competition. Don't let the grass grow under your feet or you'll be pipped to the post.

193 There are unresolved issues from the past. You would benefit from counselling or therapy. Be strong and get the help you need.

194 Stand up and be counted! Your ideas may be controversial, but you are onto a winner!

195 Sell some of your items that you no longer need. The extra cash will be extremely beneficial to you at this present time.

196   Start saving. Cut down on luxury items and be thriftier by using money saving vouchers, using up leftover food and switching to cheaper brands. Then watch your savings grow!

197   Get a good deal on a weekend break by surfing the net. That way, the relaxation and fun that's much needed will be obtainable.

198   There's a light at the end of the tunnel and by the end of the month, you'll feel happy again!

199   A business deal will come to fruition 4 weeks from today.

200   A happy outcome with your relationship makes you feel secure. Romance is in abundance so make the most of a good thing. You have found the One!

201 Mum knows best, so get some good advice from your mum or a mother figure.

202 Don't neglect things such as your accounts and money matters. Keep records up-to-date. Start a filing system, in a couple of months' time you'll be glad you did.

203 Stop getting distracted. Each time this happens, it takes you away from the task in hand and then it becomes harder and harder to motivate yourself. Regain your focus, make a schedule and stick to it. Then success will come.

204 If it isn't broken, don't try to fix it. The things in your life that are working don't need to be changed. Just change the things that aren't working for you.

205 Make an extra effort with the way you look. Get rid of old scruffy clothes and think how you present yourself to the world. This will improve your confidence and self-esteem no end.

206 There are many chances around you right now, but because you've been burying your head in the sand lately you haven't been noticing them. You still have time to turn this around.

 207 Daydream about your future whilst listening to music. Research shows that listening to music is a good way to reduce stress levels, enabling you to think more clearly.

 208 Your intuition is correct in this situation. You're seeing things clearly. Trust your instincts.

 209 Focus on your success as this is your best revenge on those who have crossed you.

 210 A wonderful and ingenious idea will soon be yours. Don't dismiss it, act upon it for huge rewards.

211 Stop being stubborn and listen to advice. Others are talking sense. Take on board their thoughts and comments.

212 Go back to basics for a while. Eat simple food and stop living beyond your means. You've been wasteful and frivolous in the past, so think of ways to make savings. You'll soon feel the benefits.

213 When making an important decision about choosing a professional to do a job, remember to ask your colleagues for a recommendation. In this scenario, word of mouth is best.

214 Organise a celebration for someone special and let your hair down. Your loved one will be happy and grateful that you did.

215 You've been hiding your feelings away, instead of saying what you think. Find your voice and express yourself.

236   Being judgemental will turn others against you. Identify your prejudices and work towards resolving them. By looking at things from a new perspective, it'll give you increased hope for the future.

 237   Walking will alleviate your dark mood, improve your thinking and alter your brain waves by releasing endorphins. Watch how your mood improves, how re-energised you feel and how much fitter you are after adopting a brisk walk into your daily routine.

 238   You're confused and are disillusioned about a situation. Think carefully before acting right now or you could end up losing a special someone.

 239   Enjoy what you have, count your blessings and see the positive aspects of your life. The more you focus on the negatives, the more you plan to fail.

 240   Find humour in the existing situation. If you can't beat them, join them! You need to have a good laugh about it and stop worrying. Things will work out just fine.

241 The situation may feel like it's hopeless, but there's a solution right around the corner. Just stay strong and know things are about to change for the better.

 242 Just remember, when your back is pushed against the wall, that's when your at your strongest. Fight like a lion and defend what's yours.

 243 Be natural and be yourself. You don't need to try too hard in this situation. Be authentic and don't try to convince someone to like you.

 244 Maintain your dignity, don't let another's harsh words bring you down. Definitely don't allow them to drag you into a bitter argument. Rise above it and maintain your power.

 245 Assert yourself: if you don't want to do something then say 'no'. Don't be persuaded to back down on this.

246 Take the reins and volunteer to do some charitable work or assist someone who is raising money for a good cause. The people you meet doing this will become close friends.

 247 You're becoming stuck in a routine. Watch your behaviour and keep a diary. See where you can implement changes.

 248 It's time to be honest with yourself and those around you. A problem you've been hiding needs to be shared with others, which will then create a solution. Take a deep breath, sit down and discuss it.

 249 It's time to delegate. You are taking on far too much and this is putting you under extreme pressure. You may feel important and useful when helping others, however it's time to allow them to take on their own responsibilities and for you to stop taking over.

 250 Friends can be a blessing, but friends can also be a pain! Don't allow yourself to be manipulated by a 'so called' friend.

251 A surprise outing comes in the form of an invitation. Keep checking your post or in-box and accept their kind offer.

 252 When a plan is coming together you'll feel happy. This is because you're aligned with your destiny.

 253 Stop thinking about yourself and your problems. To alleviate these thoughts, help out a friend in need, it will give your mood a much-needed lift.

 254 Planning a trip or day out is what you and your loved ones need. A break away to celebrate an upcoming birthday will bring happy times.

 255 Throwing yourself into the deep end will make you see that you're able to accomplish far more than you thought possible. It may be a challenge, but you can rise to the occasion.

256 You're being over sensitive in this situation. Sometimes it's best to ignore things and not respond.

257 Everything will be alright. Stay positive and focussed right now. Do not throw in the towel. Keep going for a successful outcome.

258 Enough is enough! You've been strung along by this person for far too long. Have your say then back away.

259 Sometimes to not respond puts you in a far stronger position than by fighting back. This is not cowardly, it's a sign of strength.

260 Take photographs or pictures. This will give a great impression of what you're trying to achieve. Creativity is the key aspect to this challenge.

261   You are a wonderful person, there is no denying it. You are allowing someone to exert their negative power over you. Stand up to them, no more manipulation.

 262   You are denying the truth. You are making excuses for another person's bad behaviour. Be honest with yourself about this situation as you can change it.

 263   Technology is on your side and that involves websites or self-promotion. Using the internet is a definite must for your career.

 264   Give praise where needed, especially for a friend's success. Don't feel jealous or envious, your time will come.

 265   The waiting is now over. A plan is coming together so be ready.

266 Fear makes you see things negatively and holds you back. Turn your thoughts into positive statements and verbalise them.

 267 A cat will bring healing and pleasure, welcome them in.

 268 Invitations are often opportunities in disguise. Do not turn anything down in the foreseeable future.

 269 Be caring and committed to your partner or a loved one. They're feeling neglected and need your reassurance.

 270 Travel and movement is coming. Prepare for a trip by working on a fitness routine.

271   Eat new and exciting foods, such as raw, unusual vegetables, beans and pulses. Your energy will soar.

 272   Now is a good time to draw close to animals. Take a look at rescue centres to either adopt a new pet or make a donation of your time or money.

 273   Finances are dominating your thoughts. The more you focus on the lack of money, the less you'll have. Change your thoughts into more positive feelings about your finances.

 274   Each day is a new beginning. As the sun rises, imagine you're being recharged and feeling full of energy and new vitality. Go for what you want.

 275   Cleanse and detox your body. Drink green tea and adopt a healthy new eating pattern. No snacking between meals will mean a fitter body.

276　You're like an owl, full of wisdom late at night. Write down your thoughts and ideas, then sleep on them.

277　Someone around you is displaying dishonest behaviour. Talk to this person to reveal the truth behind their actions.

278　Spend time with animals or help with an animal charity. You have love and compassion for pets. You are able to counsel people who've lost animals and who may be grieving for them.

279　It's time to detox your life. Drink plenty of herbal teas and be caffeine and sugar free for a while.

280　Feelings of depression and low moods will pass. Invigorate your life with colour by redecorating a room in your home.

281 Breakdowns and faulty items are around you. Make sure your insurance policies are up-to-date.

282 Buying an item of jewellery for someone close to you will put a smile on their face and let them know what you mean to them.

283 Ladies, throw your old make-up away and get new. Also, look at skin care routines which will make you feel younger and looking wonderful. Men, use facial scrubs and male moisturising products for instant appeal to attract a mate!

284 The letter 'J' will be meaningful right now so look out for anyone with this initial. They need you!

285 Money and finances are at risk of being overlooked. Look at ways to save your cash and even consider changing your bank account.

286   You're under a lot of pressure at the moment. Decisions need to be made, not put off.

287   Get some fresh air and exercise, a brisk walk or jog will make you feel alive.

288   An old school friend is about to get in touch, welcome them with open arms.

289   An invitation is on its way. Your initial reaction may be to refuse, but this is an opportunity in disguise.

290   Dust off your diary and make notes about a current situation. This will prove to be valuable evidence later on.

291 A certificate or award is on its way to you, see only success not failure.

 292 After a difficult month, know that the worst is behind you. In 21 days' time, good luck is on its way!

 293 Keep your friends close but your enemies closer. Be wary of someone who has an ulterior motive around you. Be especially careful if anyone asks you for money.

 294 Do not lend anything, including money, unless you can afford to lose it.

 295 Simple home cooked meals, not fast food, will give you more energy and help you to lose weight.

296   Look after your teeth, do not miss a dental appointment or check-up.

 297   You will only sleep well if you have a comfortable bed and fresh bedding. Give your bedroom a makeover, invest in a new mattress and redecorate.

 298   You're about to go on a spiritual journey. Relax and go with the flow.

 299   Check all paperwork closely before you sign your name on anything.

 300   A new project or home will be yours this year.

301 You need to reconnect with your spirit. To do this, show compassion to others less fortunate than yourself. This will make you feel whole again. Have faith, things are about to improve.

 302 You're about to receive some fantastic news and a wonderful surprise. Be gracious as you receive this and show gratitude when you share your good news with your family and friends.

 303 Ask for help. Stop trying to fix everything by yourself. Ask and you shall receive.

 304 The 17th of this month is going to be a very joy filled day. Stop worrying about results or other similar things. It's all going to be fine.

 305 Fear is consuming you and stopping you from taking that next important step. There's nothing to be afraid of. It's time to believe in yourself.

306   A friend is suffering, go and comfort them as they need your wise words and support.

 307   A feud needs to end immediately. Be the peacemaker. See things from the other person's point of view, in order to put things right.

 308   Ask yourself, "what is the right thing to do in this situation?" Then act accordingly.

 309   You're a workaholic. It's time to stop, slow down and listen to your body. A rest is needed, not just for your physical well-being but for your mental well-being too. A walk on the beach, or in the countryside will restore you.

 310   New friends and relationships will find you in the next 4 weeks. Go out and socialise, let your hair down and have fun. Old friends may go, but this makes room for new ones to come in. Stop regretting what's gone, you can't change the past. New and exciting things are on the horizon.

311 It's time to forgive. That doesn't mean that you'll forget, but by forgiving someone, you'll release yourself from bitterness and anger.

 312 Give something away today. It's even harder to give away something you love, but it'll show an important person in your life how much they mean to you.

 313 When we lose someone, we grieve. This is part of the healing process. You're coming out of the darkness now and back into the light.

 314 You have an important life mission. You have important work to do. Think of a career in nursing, teaching or a job where you will be helping many.

 315 You would make a brilliant counsellor. You have the ability to listen, understand and empathise with others.

316 Your leadership skills are needed. Stand up for yourself and those around you. Whether that's supporting a charity fundraiser or organising a work event, you can make a huge difference.

317 Stay faithful to your family and friends, especially if someone is trying to turn you against them. Your family will always support you and never let you down.

318 The person who is setting up a new home around you needs help with furnishing it. Offer any practical and material help that you can.

319 Big changes are coming next month. Don't bury your head in the sand as you need to prepare. You can move mountains if you try.

320 A legal issue needs to be tackled head on. Take professional advice and see it through to the end. Gather information, keep records and sort out paperwork for a positive outcome.

321 You are moving, a new door is about to open. This will be challenging but will bring great rewards.

 322 The next 6 weeks ahead will be much quieter and peaceful. Enjoy this tranquil time, as a very busy time will follow.

 323 Don't be shy. It's time to take the limelight. Your name will be featured in print. It's your time to shine.

 324 A loving relationship will become even stronger. Commitments and proposals will happen soon.

 325 Watch your diet and nutrition. Adopt a healthy way of eating and drinking. Within 3 weeks you will feel better than you have in ages. Watch the compliments flood in.

326 A project you never thought would get off the ground needs to be completed. It's possible to have great success with this.

 327 Within the next 2 weeks, someone you've not heard from will come back in your life. Once you get over the shock, welcome them back with open arms.

 328 It's time to embrace new challenges. A workshop or college course will change the way you look at life. It will inspire you and give you the answers you have been looking for.

 329 Using mindfulness or meditation techniques will give you clarity and answer your questions. Your subconscious mind will bring new ideas.

 330 It's time to be proactive. Update your CV and really sell yourself. Show some initiative by approaching companies that you would like to work for and a new job will soon be yours.

331 There is someone around you who has not got your best interests at heart and is trying to manipulate you. Take the moral high ground with this person, before things get out of hand.

332 Live for today and stop worrying about the future. Remember that most of the things we worry about don't even happen. You're taking life too seriously. Stop analysing everything and go and have some fun.

333 A hectic and busy time lies ahead. Courage and strength of character will be tested. The advantage to this is that you'll learn many new skills in a short space of time and will gain great life experiences. Stay calm and focussed for best results.

334 The next relationship you will encounter will be right for you. This person will be loving, loyal and kind, as they are your soul mate.

335 Read some new books or magazines to broaden your mind. A complex problem that you thought would never be resolved, will suddenly be sorted out, bringing relief to your stress.

336   Temptation is all around you. Ask yourself three questions before proceeding. Is this person worth it? Who am I hurting? What will happen if I am found out? Once you have considered these factors, then make your choice.

337   A well-earned reward or recognition of your achievements is on its way to you. Well done!

338   The sky is the limit! Ask for what you want, believe in yourself and your world will change. A successful, enchanting time is here for you.

339   A youngster needs your guidance. Act in a nurturing, parental way and guide them accordingly. You respond well to children and can create a safe haven when they need your help.

340   Your loved ones who are in heaven are still very much connected to you. Look out for the signs that they send, as these are messages to let you know that they watch over you.

341 It's time to break free and move on. Reach out and ask for help and support during this stressful time. There are many organisations that can offer help and advice, especially if you feel that you do not want to confide in family or friends. You can implement significant life changes.

342 A new baby brings happiness and light into your world.

343 A clearer path is ahead with the worst being behind you. In the month of September, you'll feel a huge sense of relief and stability. The name Jack will be helpful.

344 A financial improvement is coming to you. This will enable you to replace many of your old items. This will improve your lifestyle and the way you travel, as a shiny black car will be yours.

345 Just remember, that person who is always trying to outshine you or trying to be better than you by copying your ideas and trying to pass them off as their own is coming from a place of insecurity and is desperate for attention. Don't worry, as you'll have the last laugh.

346   You're amazing at knowing how to manifest what you need. Use your resources wisely to create a better lifestyle for yourself and family.

 347   You feel other people's pain and are a very sympathetic person. You can't rescue everyone and sometimes people need to find their own way out of problems and difficulties. Do not take away someone's opportunity to grow and learn.

 348   You are not a bottomless pit of supply. Learn how to say no and stick to it.

 349   Be a free spirit. Don't feel intimidated by others in power such as your boss etc. You do not have to conform or be a people pleaser.

 350   Take things slowly in a new romance or friendship. Get to know this person really well before making decisions or commitments.

You're a highly sensitive person who has experienced painful relationships in the past. The right person is out there for you, so don't give up and think it's never going to happen as that person will come along in the next 8 weeks.

 Travelling and seeing the world is a valuable opportunity that is going to be presented to you later in the year. Grab this opportunity with both hands. You will have an exciting adventure.

 The name 'Paul' will be instrumental in you getting a new job. This is the person that can open new doors for you.

 You have a tendency to take on other people's problems. People instinctively know that they can trust you. Even strangers will offload their problems onto you. You're a natural counsellor, so if you're looking for a new career, this would be a good path to go down.

 You're naturally clairvoyant and have your own psychic ability. Research, read or attend classes to understand this further.

356   Get some exercise to blow off some steam. Jog, run or try a yoga class or DVD. This will lift your mood and allow you to see things from a new perspective.

 357   Take a chance and stop playing it safe. Successful people take risks and they dare to dream. Allow your dreams to materialise by taking a risk on something.

 358   Fear of rejection is holding you back. You're holding on to negative comments and believing them. These comments were made by a person with very low self-esteem who was inflicting their pain onto you. Release your fears now, in order to move forward. You're a wonderful person with so much to offer.

 359   A breakthrough is about to happen. You have been working so hard and now that's about to pay off. You will be head-hunted for a new role and you're ready to accept this new challenge.

 360   Take a break from technology and, in particular, social media. Reconnect with yourself by having a countryside walk and some much-needed self-pampering.

361 When doors keep shutting in your face, know that it's the time to give up and admit defeat. Try another tactic and start again from scratch.

362 Congratulations! You're on the right path. The recent difficulties you've been dealing with are now over. Life is going to take a new and exciting turn for the better.

363 You are about to manifest what you want in your life by thinking positive thoughts with positive outcomes. Make a list of your goals and watch them materialise.

364 Relationships are out of balance at the moment. If things become heated, remove yourself from the situation and seek helpful advice.

365 You have come full circle and have completed an important stage of your life. Stop looking back, it's time to move on.

366   You're faced with a choice. Discuss your options with a trusted friend as you need to remain open minded. Weigh up all the pros and cons before you proceed.

367   Reward yourself and take pride in your accomplishments. Reflect on all you have done and how hard you've worked. You deserve a treat.

368   There is an old saying that 'things come in 3's'. You feel as though you've had your 3 strikes of bad luck already this year. It's time to look ahead now, draw a line under the past and start again.

369   Be observant. The spirit world is sending you signs. Anything that is repeated 3 times in your day, is a special message of guidance, especially if it's someone's name.

370   A new business venture is a real winner, so put your energy into this new opportunity. Be confident and charge ahead.

371   Out with the old and in with the new. This includes a new vehicle as your existing vehicle will start to require expensive repairs.

 372   There is a great deal of unfairness around you. Stand up to these bullies and make your voice heard. Enough is enough!

 373   A new pet will come into your life. Be open to receiving and welcoming them into your home.

 374   It's time for you to get some health checks. Visit the optician, dentist and even a check-up with your GP. This will improve your health and lifestyle.

 375   Put yourself into someone else's shoes as they share their problems with you. This will give you a better understanding of the issues that they face.

376 Treat yourself to a new outfit. You're going to need it as there is an invitation about to arrive and you will want to look your best on this occasion.

 377 Make a list of your financial incomings and outgoings. Stop burying your head in the sand where debt is concerned. Seek advice from the Citizen's Advice Bureau or helpful organisations. This will bring resolution to your money worries.

 378 You are suffering from a build-up of resentment from a time in your life where you were treated badly in a personal relationship. This has resulted in you feeling tired and drained as you are annoyed with yourself for allowing someone else to take advantage of your good nature.

 379 It's the strong people who seek out and accept therapy, not the weak ones.

 380 Stay connected to your family, make the effort to visit, send cards or phone family members, even the ones you have lost touch with.

381 A new project will satisfy your curiosity and need for learning new things. Researching your family tree or taking a class in something you have always wanted to do would be a positive step forward and bring new knowledge.

382 A grandparent that has gone over to the spirit world is watching over you and sending you love and healing at this time.

383 Support and advice is needed around your parents or parent right now. Keep a close eye on them, discuss any worries or concerns they may have.

384 New beginnings are here for you. You've waited a long time for this and now your patience is being rewarded. Enjoy this time of change.

385 A friend or acquaintance has had some recent good luck. You may feel a little envious of this and wish it was happening to you but remember, your chance will come.

386 If you're asked to join in with celebrations over someone else's success then make sure you accept this opportunity with grace and decorum. Being a green-eyed monster doesn't suit you.

 387 There's nothing worse than someone breaking a promise or letting you down. Don't rely on this person any longer. Start to see them as they really are.

 388 A partnership which includes a business venture is ripe for success. Take some professional advice before you sign any documents, but understand you are now moving in the right direction.

 389 A happy time is here. You're entering into a wonderful phase of your life which will be surrounded by loving people. Relationships will be particularly strong right now. You deserve to feel loved and cherished.

 390 News of a pregnancy or birth will bring great joy around you.

391   By doing some very simple and regular exercise, you'll feel your energy levels returning.

 392   An important letter in the post will bring the news you've been waiting for. You can breathe a sigh of relief, as you know that everything will be okay.

 393   After going through a difficult time, your situation is improving, especially around your health. Pay close attention to eating a healthy and varied diet to restore your vitality.

 394   The quiet phase of the recent weeks will now be followed by intense activity. Look out for the name 'Russell' as this person will not only be helpful but will be an important piece of the jigsaw as you plan ahead, and make provisions for your future.

 395   A holiday or break will do you the world of good. A change of scene, some clean air and taking it easy will reduce your stress levels.

396 Playing it safe can hinder your progress and you'll remain stuck in the familiar. Take a gamble or chance on a person or situation, and start to feel alive again.

397 An important anniversary brings memories of love but also makes you remember the emotional loss that you encountered. Be gentle on yourself and know, that as time moves on, so do you.

398 When facing a moral dilemma, it's best to stick to your guns and know that you're right. Do not ignore things. It's time to take action.

399 Good luck will be found as you walk through a green front door. Your life will then alter in a surprising but wonderful way.

400 You are at the end of a cycle or phase in your life and about to enter a new one. Someone who you perceive as an interfering busy body will actually give you some really excellent advice. Be open to listening to this and taking it on board.

401 A coastal walk will re-energise you and help you see things clearly. Your doubts will be lifted and a decision making process will follow.

 402 Look at how to make extra money instead of spending it. By clearing out your wardrobe and household items that you no longer use, your finances will be boosted. Make the effort to take your items to a car boot sale or sell on an online auction.

 403 Instead of complaining that you can't afford to buy new furniture, repaint it instead. This will unleash your creative side.

 404 You are very good at giving advice to everyone else, but you don't take your own. Alter your routine, be proactive and get out of the rut you've got yourself into.

 405 You are ready to take on a new challenge and get your teeth into something. Your positive outlook means that you will see this challenge through to the end. This will lead you out of your comfort zone but will increase your self-development.

406 A trip to London will be exciting and full of great fun and laughter, get planning now!

407 To improve your self-confidence, go clothes shopping and update your wardrobe with some modern items. Go for colours and styles that are different to your usual taste. You're going to get plenty of opportunities to wear them.

408 If a friend or friends start to treat you badly back away. They are not worth your time and effort. New and loyal friends are about to enter your life.

409 You are far more capable than you realise. Aim higher. Set yourself some goals and success will be yours.

410 Hoarding items or even your ideas are giving you a false sense of security. This will stop any progress and you'll become stale in your thoughts, and actions. Clearing the clutter and sharing your ideas without fear, will ensure a new wave of prosperity.

411 Look out for a strong male figure coming into your life. This man will have the initial 'R'. He will bring fun and laughter as you connect with him.

 412 Safety first. Do not ignore house maintenance or car service checks. It's easy to keep putting these things off when you are busy, so pencil them into your diary.

 413 A huge amount can be achieved in just one day. Get up early and tackle all the jobs you keep putting off.

 414 Being frugal can make a significant difference to your finances. Take some time to go through your bills and outgoings and see where savings can be made. Switching energy suppliers and credit card balances can make life easier.

 415 Savings can be made by searching for best prices online, using money saving vouchers or even making packed lunches. Put these savings to one side, as it will soon add up and allow you to take a break or day out.

416 The name of Mark or Martin will be in touch with you within the next 4 weeks. Listen to what they have to say and accept it. Keep calm and go with your gut instinct about how to move forward with this person.

417 This feud needs to stop now before someone gets physically or emotionally scarred. It's time to wave the white flag and offer an olive branch of forgiveness.

418 Instead of feeling envious of someone around you, congratulate them instead. This will turn the tables and they'll become a very helpful friend and ally.

419 It's easy to feel dispirited when your good ideas keep being knocked down by another person. Caustic remarks are lowering your self-esteem. Pick yourself up by talking to someone who is fair and non-judgemental as they will enable you to see things from a new perspective.

420 The quandary that you find yourself in is disengaging you from your usual lust for life. Know that things are now moving towards a conclusion and your happy-go-lucky nature will return in the next 2 months.

421 Seeking out new friendships by joining a group of like-minded people will require some courage. This will be well worth it as the person you meet with the initial 'J' for their first name, will have a huge impact on your life.

422 A family member whose birthday is in the month of June needs guidance and understanding. They are faced with a dilemma and with your compassionate nature and level head, you can advise them accordingly.

423 Your dreams of living an idyllic lifestyle in a wonderful place will come true in the future. It's easy to give up on our dreams when we're having a hard time, but dreams really can come true.

424 A simple action of sending a text, email or making a phone call to someone you haven't heard from for a while will make their day and show them that they are important and meaningful in your life.

425 A lucrative business idea needs further exploration. This could be the answer to your prayers, lead to your independence and give you a feeling of self-worth. All you need now is a positive attitude and some motivation. By next Christmas, you'll be well on your way to an exciting future.

426 Look back through old notebooks and memorabilia to find a gem of an idea that you had forgotten about. It's relevant in your life today and in the future. This will send you off in a new direction.

 427 A close friend is going to disclose a secret and confidential information. Do not be shocked as they make this confession, but be caring and supportive.

 428 Never a loaner or borrower be. Remember these wise words when you are asked to lend someone a significant amount of money. If you can afford to lose this money, then lend it, but remember, not only will you never see this money again, you'll also never see the borrower again!

 429 Think very carefully before you have a tattoo, as you will regret this very quickly. If this does not apply directly to you, then show this message to someone around you who is about to go and see a tattoo artist. Stop and think before you/they commit.

 430 You require the love and healing that you can only get from pets. Consider having a pet in your life and remember there are many animals in rescue shelters that would make a great companion.

431 Taking someone to court can feel like a huge challenge and a last resort. This person needs to face what they have done and be stopped, as their actions are unacceptable. Be strong and assert yourself. It will be a moral triumph on your part.

432 Reckless spending will only give you the feel good factor for a short time but will leave you in a considerable amount of debt. Return any items for a refund and curb that spending now.

433 You are making huge progress even if you think you're not. Your life is starting to speed up from the end of this month. Make sure you become very organised. Sort out paperwork and reorganise your shelves and cupboards. Things you thought you'd lost will re-emerge.

434 Stop judging those around you and appreciate what good people you have in your life. You've become a little disillusioned with what's going on. A reality check is needed.

435 See through the person with the condescending attitude when they speak to you, as they are hurting inside. Instead of avoiding them, do the opposite and ask them to join you for a drink or meal. They will then show you gratitude and confide in you.

436 Accept you can't always have everything you want and not everyone will dance to your tune. You need to back down and get off your high horse. Listen to others people's points of view.

 437 Instigate a meeting or outing with friends or family or even hold a party. Instead of waiting to be invited to events, create your own and you'll have lots of fun doing so.

 438 Instead of resisting change, embrace it. Of course it's natural to feel apprehensive but unless you take a risk and go for it, you'll never know what possibilities await.

 439 Having a rival can be an extremely positive thing. This will inspire and motivate you to do better. A challenge lies ahead in a very competitive way and you can win hands down!

 440 Rome was not built in a day and the project you're working on is a process. Each stage takes time to complete. If you rush you will make mistakes.

441 You're so busy running around that you're not listening to your inner self and intuition. Your mind has become cluttered, so it's no wonder you're finding it hard to make decisions. Still your mind by taking a walk out in nature or by participating in meditation.

442 You have acquired all the tools and information you need to proceed. You're far stronger than you realise and are fiercely independent. Use these attributes and defend what's yours.

443 The situation you're asking about requires you to be versatile and remain flexible. You're going through a period of transformation where you will emerge a far stronger and wiser person for this experience.

444 This number reminds you that happiness is going to be yours for the taking. Good relationships, buoyant finances and new opportunities will fill your heart with joy.

445 You've longed for some peace and quiet in your life but when you get it you become bored and lonely. Enjoy and appreciate some time away from friends and family. Use this time wisely by reading and nurturing your creativity.

446   It's time for a reality check where your health and fitness is concerned. Look at eating a healthy diet and cut down on any alcohol and caffeine rich drinks.

447   Don't take anything for granted. Be grateful and appreciate all the positive things in your life. You have a capacity for feeling sorry for yourself. To counteract this, be grateful for what you've got and you'll recognise just how far you've come.

448   It's far easier to blame others for what we feel is wrong in our life. Stop reliving the past. It's time to accept what has happened, reach closure and to move on.

449   If you feel nothing is happening then make something happen! Use your abilities to create movement in areas of your life that feel dormant. So, if you need a new job, either become self-employed or take initiative and approach companies you would like to work for. Push yourself forward and within 1 month you will have unlocked a new opportunity.

450   Change the patterns of your behaviour and routine and your life will change. You've become stuck in a rut, so it's time to break free.

It's time to offload and release your anger and blame. A friend with an empathetic nature will encourage a conversation where you'll be able to talk openly about a situation that upset you immensely. It's safe to open up and you will feel a sense of relief that you've been able to confide in someone.

 Nothing stays the same. Your situation is about to change for the better. This change will be emotional, but you won't look back.

 Although you're under a great deal of pressure, remember to maintain a calm persona around others. People look up to you and feel safe and secure when you're around, so stay in control.

 Extra help and support is needed right now. Don't put off asking for help and assistance. Face your fears, be brave and then things will improve tremendously.

 A new interest in spiritual and healing work sees you connecting with some very influential people. This will also lead to travelling to different areas of the country. An exciting time lies ahead.

456 A time of luck and good fortune is with you for the next 3 months. Enter competitions and prize draws whilst in this lucky phase. Synchronicity will also place you in the right place at the right time for meetings with useful people. The name 'Peter' will also be lucky for you.

457 A conversation around the subject of fostering or adoption will bring revelations and a whole new meaning to your life or someone close to you. Research is needed in this area.

458 Making peace with someone who has caused great anguish and upset is no easy feat. Now is the right time to put the past behind you and let bygones be bygones.

459 Research natural healing remedies such as acupuncture, Bach flower remedies, Reiki healing and other methods. These can bring great relief and re-energise you.

460 A strong male is coming into your life. What is wonderful is that he has a relaxed nature and a great sense of humour. You'll form a close connection and bond immediately.

461 A new baby will grace yourself or someone close to you. This child will be very special indeed and will bring so much happiness.

 462 A solution to an ongoing problem is here. Things will now be sorted out in the next 4 weeks to your satisfaction.

 463 When we embark on an important project or start something new, it's easy to forget what questions to ask. Sit down quietly and make a list of all the significant questions before you have any meetings. This will give you all the answers you seek.

 464 It's time to make a stand and to also make a commitment to yourself or another. Knuckle down and work hard. This will have a huge bearing on the next 2 years of your life. You'll then reap the rewards.

 465 New romance is on its way. You're now ready to accept love and commitment into your life. Don't be scared, this is the right person for you.

466 Stop biting your tongue! It's time to have your say. You have bottled things up for far too long. It's now safe to speak your mind.

467 You are a natural clairvoyant and are able to predict the future through visions and pictures in your mind. This gift needs understanding so take time to join a class or attend a spiritualist church for support and guidance.

468 Revealing information will come to you from an unexpected source. Use this information wisely and act upon it.

469 You have a free spirit that longs to be let loose. Make plans to go on an adventure, this may be a trip or even trying a new sport. You will feel exhilarated and become an adrenalin junkie!

470 Look for some calm in all of the chaos. A short break can restore you and your depleted energy levels.

471 It's time to pick out and choose new items and décor for your home. This place can really be exactly what you've dreamed of.

472 You're about to experience a breakthrough. The next 6 weeks will be pivotal in progressing a business idea. Make sure people know about your idea or product. Social media will help bring awareness to your business.

473 Obstacles which have been blocking your progress are now being removed. Paperwork will need signing, so make sure you read the small print and then go and celebrate.

474 Not all the people in your life have your best interests at heart. You are often too nice to say no to these people and therefore you allow them to make unfair demands on your time and energy. It's time to assert yourself and learn how to refuse and say no.

475 During this difficult time, put a brave face on things. You need to be the strong one and to lift others' spirits. Show your compassionate side and be supportive.

476   Just be there for a friend who really needs you right now. It's not always about the words you say, it's more about the actions you show.

477   Everything's going to be alright. You've been worrying and over complicating things lately. It's now time to stop and relax.

478   The answer to your question is 'yes'. Go ahead, go forward, just do it!

479   Be gracious and accept the invitation that's on offer, even if you feel like refusing. It'll prove to be a very good decision.

480   The answer to your question is 'no'. It's just not the right time, wait for better results.

481 Your body is craving exercise, movement and even dance. Ideally, join a class or club but if this is not possible, exercise at home.

482 Keep going and do not give in. Your goal is now within reach. Keep moving forwards in order to achieve.

483 You are becoming stuck in a rut, so it's time to expand your horizons. Explore a new place or book onto a college course. The options are endless and new, fun experiences lie ahead.

484 The 21st day of the next month will be a time of closure for you. Put the past behind you and start afresh.

485 Two heads are better than one. Work alongside a trusted friend to accomplish a lifelong ambition.

486 Destiny sees you in your very own shop. A retail business opportunity will bring financial security and allow you to be your own boss.

 487 We all have regrets and we have all done something we're ashamed of. Reflect on this and admit you were wrong, then put it behind you and stop sabotaging yourself.

 488 A cash injection is on its way to you. Do not waste it, spend it wisely.

 489 If you take bitter revenge on someone, it'll just lead to your own destruction. Just trust in karma and this person will get what's coming to them.

 490 Decisions need careful consideration. Do not rush into anything as there is a better option ahead. Bide your time for another 3 weeks, then go for it.

491 Accept the way things are for now. If everything you want to happen happened straight away you would never cope. So remember, patience is a virtue and things will change in due course.

492 Remember there is always hope for the future. When you are caught up in a difficult situation or dealing with someone who is, take time out to reassure yourself that things will improve.

493 Memories are special and are a way for you to stay connected with loved ones that we miss dearly. By talking about them, looking at photographs or even keeping a memory box with some sentimental objects inside can help us deal with our loss.

494 It's hard to forgive and to show forgiveness, especially when someone has hurt us deeply and made us angry. Holding on to this pain is restricting you from moving forward with your life and spoiling new relationships. Seek counselling or confide in a well trusted friend and release those negative emotions.

495 Give away something that means a lot, this will prove how much a loved one means to you. Concentrate on doing one good deed each week without expecting anything in return. By focussing on kindness and assisting others it'll put you on your true path of self discovery.

496 The end of an era in your life is about to happen. This will stir up feelings of sadness but also of being treated unfairly. This can lead to you feeling anxious and even depressed. To combat this, fight back and defend yourself. By June 10th-12th, things will have changed for the better and new offers will flood in.

 497 Stop and think before you proceed. This is not the right time to rush into any decision making process. More research is required.

 498 The next month is full of surprises, especially with chance meetings with people you haven't seen for some time. Make sure you ask them for their phone number or contact details so that you can stay in touch.

 499 You are about to go through a major life change. Stay calm and hopeful during this period of uncertainty. As the dust settles and you re-establish yourself, you'll realise that this was the best solution for everyone. A much happier time lies ahead. August will be a time of fun and adventure.

 500 New beginnings are here at last. All your hard work is about to pay off. This is a time of financial security where debts will be settled and you will feel free and excited about the future. As you move forward and become more courageous, you're no longer going to allow fear to hold you back. Life is for living, go and celebrate your good fortune.

501 Dreams can come true, you just need a little bit of courage and determination to see the pot of gold at the end of the rainbow.

502 A celebration will bring family and friends together. This will heal old wounds and allow bygones be bygones.

503 Trust your instincts about that new person that's just come into your life. They are NOT all that they seem.

504 You are giving up on a dream too early! You believe that you've exhausted every avenue but you're wrong. This situation can be turned around, you just need advice from the right person, so keep searching and the answer will follow.

505 You have made your decision and now is the time to execute it. Stop putting it off, take action now.

506 In 7 days from now your life will change. This may be an unexpected event or from a piece of information that's divulged to you. Regard this as a positive step forward.

507 There are many aspects to your life that you are doing just because you feel you 'should'. Make a list of what these are. Then look at how you can stop being a people pleaser and you will see your life in a different way.

508 The 11th day of the following month is extremely lucky for you. Take a chance, be courageous and go for it.

509 Ask yourself these 3 questions: Am I in the right career? Do I enjoy my job? Am I fulfilled in my work? If you answer no to one or more of these, then it's time to do something about it.

510 By keeping a food diary, you can track the amount of sugar, wheat and caffeine in your diet. Substitute these for healthy alternatives. Your body will respond positively by giving you more energy and vitality.

Someone close to you is extremely manipulative and criticises you constantly. Now is the time to stand up to them but before you do, confide in a good friend or helpful person that you trust. With their support you can become more assertive and address this issue.

Money is slipping through your fingers. Become the master of your finances by checking your bank statements and bills. Look at where you can make savings e.g. by changing energy suppliers or moving to a 0% credit card. Research is required.

You have so many good qualities yet you seldom believe in your own capabilities. Ask 3 friends or colleagues to write down your three strengths. Focus on them regularly. This will shift your view of yourself.

Stop trying to seek someone's approval and stop worrying over what others think of you. Accept yourself for who you are. The reason you seek others' approval stems from childhood. Think back to who made you feel this way, e.g. a parent, a teacher etc. You're no longer a child, the only approval you need is your own.

Instead of resisting the changes that are around you, go with the flow. Embrace what's happening, there is no need to fear it.

516 You are doing the best you can with the resources you have. Keep going for another few weeks with the knowledge that a new beginning will change your outlook on life.

 517 You are stuck in a pattern of behaviour and routine that you've now outgrown. This has resulted in boredom and frustration. It's time to come out of your comfort zone and be more spontaneous.

 518 A new vehicle will be life changing, giving you your freedom. Look out for vehicles that are royal blue or lime green when making your decision.

 519 A meeting with a male by the name of 'Darren' will give you all the information you need and will advise you accordingly.

 520 You are letting the past hold you back. Don't allow yourself to be a victim any longer. The past is now a memory, it's time to release yourself and move on. It's therapeutic to write a letter or a list of what happened to you and then destroy it, allowing the emotional attachments to go with it.

521 Grandparents are very important to you. Make time for them and if they're no longer with you, know they watch over you from the spirit world.

 522 It's important to reconnect with family members, especially those who you have not heard from for a while. Look out for a family member making contact and reaching out to you.

 523 New romance is on its way, be ready. Buy a new outfit, get your hair done and pamper yourself. This will happen in the next 4 weeks.

 524 Animals and pets need your help and assistance right now. Reach out to assist any charities or good causes and also check the health and well-being of your own pets or any around you.

 525 You have many wonderful qualities and being a compassionate healer is one of them. You're being guided to listen and comfort someone close to you.

526 Encourage someone's talent. This person needs to be on stage and in the public eye. They have low self-esteem and that needs building up before they're able to take the next step. You can make a huge difference to them.

527 An invitation to the races or large social gathering is an opportunity too good to miss. Get your name on the list, as you are in for an awesome time.

528 A street or person's name that sounds like 'Lombard' is going to play an important role in your future career. Remember this, and look out for it in 6 weeks' time.

529 Before you rush into a medical procedure including cosmetic surgery or having a tattoo etc., talk it through with a trustworthy person or you could regret this decision at a later date.

530 It's time to forgive that person that caused you heartache and trauma. Take a piece of notepaper and write their name on it and what you're forgiving them for. Now fold it up, hold it on your heart and say to yourself 'I'm ready to let go'. Dispose of this note, you'll feel a sense of relief and closure.

531   Enter as many competitions as you can, as a prize to a holiday destination is heading your way.

532   The forename or surname of 'James' is going to come into your life. They will bring plenty of help and positivity that you'll feel like your true authentic self once more.

533   It's time to do plenty of research and to make notes and lists. You are entering a cycle in your life where you can start your own business. The month of February will be perfect for this.

534   It's time to learn to love yourself as you are your own worst critic. Appreciate your strengths, your body and your intelligence. In the past, you've settled for second best. This is a time where you can learn from your past experiences and honour yourself. Choose to walk a new path with people that are honest and genuine.

535   Stop living in chaos and disorder and become proactive. Set yourself a small challenge every day e.g. to sort out a cupboard or shelf. Then you'll feel ready to tackle larger tasks such as sorting out a room. Paint and decorate your surroundings and you'll have a home you'll feel proud of.

536 It's time to take back your power. Stop those thoughts that make you feel that you're not good enough. Remember you're worthy and you deserve better.

537 Become an assertive person and start saying, 'No'. People are taking advantage of you. Only say, 'Yes' to things that you feel are fair and make you happy.

538 You may feel as though you don't have enough time to take on a new hobby or pastime. Think about what you used to enjoy as a child, e.g. painting, horse riding, acting etc. Then look for a club or course in your area and incorporate this into your life.

539 Sit down, turn off any distractions such as the TV or radio. Close your eyes and do some deep breathing, telling yourself there is nothing to worry about. Then think about what you would like to achieve in the next 6 months. Set 2 goals for each month, whether you feel they are achievable or not. Open your eyes and write them down. Tick them off your list as you complete them.

540 Arrange a meeting with someone who you wish to have a heart to heart conversation with. Be very honest and tell them exactly how you feel.

541 Who is around you that has a long lost child that they have no contact with? This child will want to contact them soon, so be there to support and mediate.

542 The name Jack or Jackie will be someone very important to you. Make sure you stay connected and make an effort to stay in touch.

543 Wedding plans are in the air. Happy times lie ahead. Enjoy the preparation but remember, you don't have to spend a fortune to have a magical day.

544 If you find yourself feeling lonely or isolated, do not allow it to make you feel sad and frustrated. Seek out the company of like-minded individuals. Try websites such as 'Meet Up' to see what groups are in your area.

545 If you find yourself engaged in arguments, quarrels and fall-outs, remember that this won't last long and things will blow over (whether you win or lose). Just forget the whole thing and move on.

546 Look at what's going right in your life instead of focussing on what's going wrong. If you find this difficult then sit down and make a list of all the positive aspects. This will help shift your perspective into a new way of thinking.

547 You should not be apprehensive about taking decisive action. If you're too hesitant it'll impede your progress. Go forward with confidence and take matters into your own hands.

548 You're in a strong position to influence others. Make sure you're compassionate and understanding of their needs before you proceed with advice.

549 Let your intuition and your positive emotional responses guide you. Analyse carefully what others have to say and this will help you decipher the truth in this matter.

550 You need to review your health and most importantly your diet. Avoid processed foods, hidden sugars and look at reducing your gluten and wheat intake. Sticking to this plan and introducing plenty of fresh fruit and vegetables will see you losing weight and feeling full of energy.

551 Harmony is coming into your personal relationships. You've been through a tough time in the past and now it's time to enjoy earthly pleasures and material comforts.

 552 Be confident but diplomatic in financial matters. An important decision around money is only 5 weeks away. By being organised and prepared, things will go very well indeed.

 553 Share your knowledge with others. Hold workshops, write a book/manual or offer your advice. People will benefit from your words of wisdom.

 554 Your close friend or partner needs encouragement and reassurance as they're feeling low and unmotivated. Listen to their words carefully about how they see themselves and why they feel the way they do. Support them through this phase and let them know that life will change for the better.

 555 It's time to take a chance or a risk on something that you truly believe in. Take action now or you will look back with regret.

556 Be aware of being too possessive. Resist temptation, especially about squandering money. This will only make you feel good in the short term. It's time to get to the root of the problem and why you are behaving in this way.

557 Do not take part in malicious gossip just to fit in with the crowd. Be strong and independent. You will earn far more respect that way.

558 You'll be earning the position of authority in the next 2 months. Have a brave and energetic approach to this. You are ready for this challenge.

559 With power comes great responsibility. Your victory should not involve a ruthless attitude towards other people. Don't let this achievement go to your head.

560 Although you feel worried and anxious about a forthcoming situation, you're being called upon to be brave and have an energetic approach to tackling this. Be reassured that things will go to plan .

561 Be wary of someone around you who demonstrates immature behaviour in order to win and get their own way. If you're unable to steer clear of them, then show your disapproval and don't tolerate it.

 562 It's time to set a good example to those around you. Stop breaking the rules and look at the value of your own integrity.

 563 Your mind is full of superficial thoughts about things which don't really matter. Focus your mind on more important issues. Don't live in denial, start tackling your problems immediately.

 564 When embarking on a new love affair, get to know this person really well before rushing in. You're at risk of becoming infatuated with somebody as you fall in love too easily. This will result in scaring them off if you come on too strongly.

 565 Have faith in yourself as victory can be found through self-awareness. Success will come through a combination of hard work and being optimistic. Do not be scared of pushing yourself to your full intellectual capacity.

566 It's time to be fair and reasonable. Being angry and hot-headed is not the way forward, when trying to reach a conclusion concerning an ongoing argument or dispute.

567 Stop sitting on the fence. It's time to make that important decision. Do not dwell on it any longer as worry can be self-defeating.

568 You are coming to the end of a problematic period in your life. Your circumstances will now change for the better.

569 Be very alert and do not let your guard down for the next 21 days. This is because you have a rival working against you. In order to combat this, you need to raise your game, especially around work and business.

570 It's the end of an era. Accept the need for change and do not try to obstruct its course. Most of this change will come about through fate and it will be to your advantage.

A current relationship is about to deepen and love will blossom. This is a very emotional time for you as you are feeling apprehensive about taking the next step. Stop reflecting on the past and enjoy what you have now, a happy time lies ahead.

You're not trapped, you just think you are. Don't be tempted into lazy and destructive ways such as drinking or addictive behaviours. You are liked and more respected than you realise. If your life is not the way you want it, you have a forthcoming opportunity to change things for the better.

Your outlook is bright and you're continually becoming psychologically stronger. This is a good time to make firm decisions about your future.

Do not allow your inhibitions to obstruct your progress. Be determined as you deserve better. Trust in a true friend as they will listen to your fears and help you see things from a more balanced point of view. You have so much to offer, especially when working with needy people.

Do not let emotions affect your judgement and be careful not to over-react in a situation. Take a step back and reconsider.

576 You are getting a second chance, so make sure you get everything right this time. However, don't become complacent. Make a conscious effort to be more considerate and understanding.

 577 Your efforts are about to be rewarded. You will use your worldly knowledge wisely to help yourself and those around you. This is the end of a journey and it's time to let your hair down and enjoy yourself.

 578 It's time to become more humanitarian. You will benefit from being less resentful and more sympathetic. You need to forgive and forget, then your life will take a much more positive turn.

 579 A strong well-educated male is about to enter your life. He will be creative and artistic and will hold down a purposeful job. Reach out to him when you meet.

 580 An important invitation is on its way to you. It will involve travel and a new outfit, but it'll certainly be worth making the effort to attend.

Be aware that someone in your friendship circle has a tendency to lean towards addictive behaviours. This may include gambling, drinking etc. Be prepared to speak to them about this and to encourage them to seek help.

Be willing to confront problems directly, instead of sweeping them under the carpet. You've become too preoccupied with other situations around you and you've let your own difficulties mount up. Tackle one or two things daily and things will quickly resolve themselves.

It's time to calm down and watch your temper! You're feeling frustrated and confused over an issue, but progress will be slow if you approach this matter in an angry way. Rational calm thinking and communicating clearly will get you good results.

When planning a trip in the next 3 months, remember that plenty of research can make the difference between an enjoyable time or a miserable one. Don't leave things to chance.

Problems will be generated by idle gossip. Find out the facts first before you make a comment, as things are not all as they seem.

586 A change in finances will be coming your way. This could be from an unexpected gift, inheritance or a bonus at work. Invest this money wisely, do not be tempted to go on a crazy shopping spree.

587 Joining together with a good friend or family member will bring about a union of ideas. Use your initiative to come up with interesting business ideas. This will give you the motivation to start something new.

588 A profitable partnership with original money-making ideas is a real winner. Do not delay in making this a reality.

589 Someone from your past is about to make contact. Listen to what they have to say before you cast judgement.

590 Being involved in a variety of projects can be exhausting. You find it hard to say no when you are asked to assist, as this makes you feel guilty. But it's time to put yourself and your own needs first. This is not selfish, it's just about you recharging your batteries.

591 Sadness surrounds a law suit or divorce. See this through to completion in the knowledge that you are doing the right thing. Hold your head up high through this process and know that there is plenty of support around you.

592 Over tiredness can reduce vitality and promote discontent. This is due to poor quality sleep and disruptive sleeping patterns. By changing the layout of your bedroom, introducing calm colours and pictures as well as using lavender before you go to bed, you'll notice things will improve.

593 Delays and difficulties have made you feel fraught and frustrated. Persistence will win through so don't give up and keep pushing ahead. It'll be worth it in the end.

594 You have a temptation to buy more than you need and to hoard. Sit in solitude and think about why this is the case. Look to the past about what you've lost or who you're grieving for. Once you've identified this, it'll be easier to de-clutter your environment.

595 Being too impulsive during the next 2 weeks can lead to error! Think any decisions through very carefully before you make them, especially where personal relationships are concerned.

596 Success is on its way and you will be compensated for any losses you have incurred. Great relief and happiness will follow.

597 At last you're going to start enjoying your work instead of dreading it. Things will really turn around for you in 6 weeks' time. New beginnings will lead to security and success.

598 Trust your intuition. You need to get a sense of which pathway feels right for you. You have an incredible inner wisdom, so make the forthcoming decision by trusting your own instincts.

599 Stop thinking about the long-term outcome and concentrate on what is going on now. Even if things do not turn out exactly how you want them to, there will be plenty to celebrate.

600 It's time to lighten up. You've been taking life too seriously. Remember, when problems come your way, you handle things well. Book a day out, a trip to the theatre or go and see a stage show, it will lift your spirits.

601 It's time to come out of your comfort zone. Enlist on a personal challenge, whether it's running a marathon, making a speech, or visiting a new place. By doing this. It'll open the door to you having more fun and excitement in your life.

 602 Remember 'like attracts like', so by behaving in an upbeat and positive way you'll attract similar people into your friendship circle. You might need to make the first move, so invite a friend out for lunch or to an event. Do not fear rejection.

 603 Search your local newspapers, libraries or the internet for activities that you can participate in. Be willing to go to these activities alone, that way you'll reach out and meet new friends.

 604 You are caught up in a circle of worry. This has caused you to feel stressed and anxious. Remember, most things we worry about never even happen. To break this cycle, introduce relaxation techniques into your life e.g. meditation and mindfulness. Talk to a trusted friend about how you feel.

 605 Feelings of anger and blame are a result of you either being left out or being asked to leave a role that you once loved. This can lead to feelings of rejection but remember, this change will turn into a blessing.

606 News of a happy event is coming in the next few days. This will boost everyone concerned. Feelings of relief will follow.

607 You get back what you put in, therefore a small donation to a charity is appropriate. This can include clothing, household items or even a financial contribution.

608 A difficult domestic situation is coming to an end. You will be required to tackle the problem head on and this needs you to stay calm and level headed. Trust in your own ability to make the right choices.

609 Jealousy is a destructive emotion and can only lead to upset and disappointment. The root of these feelings are insecurity and low self-worth. Think of who is around you right now that displays this behaviour and reach out to them.

610 Further study will stimulate the mind and ultimately improve finances. Do not delay in enrolling on a course and trust in your own ability to make this a success.

611 It can be extremely upsetting when we lose a friend, especially when we feel we've done nothing to deserve it. Remember, they have their own issues to deal with. Move forward in the knowledge that new friends are on their way.

612 A solution to a current problem is here at last. Happy family life will resume as a result of this. Enjoy this time and celebrate with those you love.

613 You are a warm and affectionate person who is always willing to help others. You have a generous spirit and want to help and heal those around you. Be wary though, as someone is taking advantage of your good nature.

614 A question or opportunity needs serious thought. Study the evidence carefully but do not allow your emotions to cloud your decision-making process.

615 Somebody in your environment is trying to use your present situation to take advantage. Think carefully about their motives and about how genuine they are. If you give them an inch, they will take a mile, so be cautious.

616 The roller-coaster ride that you feel you've been on lately is not permanent and things will soon settle down. Look out for the name of 'Adam', he will help you greatly.

617 Reject any offer of easy money as this could backfire. Instead, work hard and concentrate on your own success. Do not be dragged down by another's negativity.

618 November is going to be a very creative month for you, so be very optimistic as your creations and crafts can be extremely profitable. Make sure you exploit your natural talents to the full.

619 It's time to take responsibility for your own actions and to stop relying on others to bail you out. This childish behaviour is disrespectful and damaging to your own personal development.

620 Do not let others dictate to you about your physical body and how you should look. Remember, you are worthy and attractive so make a decision to love yourself.

621 You do not need approval from others, you just think you do. It's time to stand up for yourself and make your own choices and decisions.

622 Sometimes it's easier to do something that you've been putting off, than to keep making excuses for why you haven't done it. Bite the bullet and get on with it.

623 You're caught up in a trap partly of your own making. Now is a good time to break free. Don't let your fear of failing become strong enough to prevent you from trying.

624 Stop allowing your past to shape your future. The past is dictating to you about how you should behave. It's time to make some positive changes, including trying new things. If you embrace the new, your future will be bright and you can wave goodbye to the restrictions of the past.

625 You have reached the stage in your life where you are ready to explore and go on a spiritual journey or retreat. The stresses of the last few weeks have worn you out, so plan a relaxing trip.

626

History can and will repeat itself unless you speak up for yourself now. You may be feeling downtrodden but ask yourself this question, "Whose fault is that?" The answer is yours! Decide to do something powerful today.

627

Age can be restrictive in some matters but not in your case. Stop worrying about how others perceive you. Remember you are beautiful, caring, kind and above all, genuine. So allow others to get to know the real you and your self-image will follow.

628

Stop rejecting compliments aimed at you. Instead say "thank you", and accept them gracefully, this will allow your confidence to be boosted.

629

You feel guilty about buying things for yourself, is this because you feel you're not worth it? You are sacrificing your own happiness and material needs to please another and in turn you are sending out all the wrong messages.

630

You will find the love of your life and marry them. Before this happens, you'll have to consciously stop putting yourself down. Once you adopt a strong and positive view, many opportunities for true love will come into your life.

631 Chasing perfection will only lead to deep dissatisfaction. Your goals need to be realistic and achievable. If not you are just setting yourself up to fail. It's time to review yourself and your life and to introduce attainable expectations that will lead to success.

 632 Life can feel like a pressure cooker at times and this is why you feel so helpless. Make a list of what factors in your life are making you feel powerless and give them a score of 1-10 (10 being the things that create the most pressure). Then look at how you can reduce the factors that score highest, e.g. by going to see your GP, delegating jobs or becoming more proactive. This shows that you're taking back your power and that you're on the road to change.

 633 At last life is starting to look rosy again. All your hard work, planning and sacrifices are leading to a much more stable and successful future.

 634 You are not alone, many people genuinely care about you and your welfare. An unexpected phone call will prove that in the next few days.

 635 Put yourself out to help someone who wouldn't normally ask for it. This act of kindness will open a door to an exciting opportunity for you. The 12th of September will see the start of great learning achievements. Make room on your mantelpiece to display an award.

636 Choosing to bury your head in the sand won't resolve a problem that is taking over your thoughts and making you feel miserable. All that is needed is a little bit of courage and determination. Talking to a relevant professional will get thing resolved more easily than you thought.

637 Your feelings of agitation and restlessness are preparation for the changes that are about to take place after 6th July. There will be a few obstacles to overcome before this, but the way ahead is bright and fulfilling, especially around work and relationships.

638 The name 'Dean' will be someone who you will want to be close to in the next few months. Not only will they have a sensitive side, but they'll be spontaneous and add some va-va-voom into your relationship. Have fun!

639 Put things into perspective and stop blowing things out of proportion. Think about how you can solve the current issue instead of being a drama queen!

640 You have adopted a very sceptical attitude to a new friend that has recently come into your life. Get to know them better and instead of being suspicious of their motives, let your guard down as they have a lot to offer.

641 By eliminating jealousy and viewing it as a negative emotion, you will stop comparing yourself to others. Therefore, you can start to value yourself more and trust in your own abilities.

 642 The tables will turn in your favour in this current situation. Stay calm and do not allow the other person to ruffle your feathers. You will come out on top!

 643 By researching your family tree, you will uncover a surprising family secret. Once you get over the shock and share this information with other family members, you'll find an uncanny way to use this to your advantage.

 644 News of an unexpected pregnancy is on the way. This really is good news and remember pink is for girls. Make a list of your favourite names, as this could be an early arrival.

 645 In the next 4 weeks, you are going to find out who your true friends are and it may not be the ones who you expect. Do not listen to their excuses. They are merely a ruse to win you around.

646 Having to deal with disappointment is never easy and often upsetting. This was a blessing in disguise. Another opportunity will be arriving on your doorstep in the next 14 days, which will supersede your last experience and fulfil your expectations.

 647 By expecting another person to take care of you puts you into 'child mode' and although it can feel like a safe place to be, you open yourself up to manipulation and not being responsible for yourself. Therefore losing your own independence and self-reliance. Turn this around by taking on more adult responsibilities such as paying your own bills and making your own decisions.

 648 Stop deluding yourself that you're happy and comfortable in this current situation. Identify who, or what, is holding you back by discussing this with a trusted friend or mentor. Agencies such as the Citizen's Advice Bureau can also be beneficial here.

 649 When looking for a new property or home remember the early bird catches the worm. Register your interest on websites and with local property experts. In 12 weeks' time, you'll be faced with a choice of 2 properties, go with your heart, not with your head.

 650 Do not give up or give in. You're almost there so don't quit. Take a deep breath and know you are capable and do have the resources to see this task through to the end.

651 You're that caught up with your busy lifestyle that you're losing touch with all the things you love in life, such as being in nature and interacting with animals. Make room in your diary to go for a walk at least once a week. This will very quickly result in relaxation and rejuvenation and even meeting new friends.

652 Stresses and strains can result in tense muscles and anxious feelings. Talking about what is going on in your life is therapeutic and will make you view things from a more balanced perspective. Alternative therapies such as Reiki healing or a massage can help restore your body and mind.

653 When looking for an expert or professional person in the next 10 days, look out for the name of 'Jenkins'. This will prove to be helpful and informative.

654 Nurture your creativity by embracing a new project or activity. A trip to your local library will reveal just what you are looking for, even if you are unsure of what it is yet.

655 When you walk into the room that smells of fresh paint and lavender, you know you've come home. Trust your instincts and act without delay.

656 Keeping secrets from those you love is never a good thing to do. Find the time to confess all and you'll find comfort and support from those around you.

657 Are you able to forgive and forget? Unless you can put your hand on your heart and truly leave things in the past without throwing things back their face, then yes, you're ready. If not, consider walking away.

658 We all make mistakes and wish we had handled things differently in certain circumstances. Stop persecuting yourself over things you cannot change. It's time to move forward without a self-sabotaging attitude. It's time to be full of optimism about your future.

659 Trust can make or break a relationship. When you find yourself rifling through a partner's pockets, checking their phone or emails then it's time to admit there's a problem.

660 Think carefully when writing a speech or an important handwritten letter. The words you use need to be mindfully chosen and written from the heart.

There is someone around you that has been a victim of severe bullying in the past. Although they have survived this harrowing ordeal they would benefit tremendously from your well-balanced listening ear. Make time for them and listen without judgement.

Stay calm when faced with a court or legal battle. Keeping your composure is key here in order to attain a favourable outcome.

Foreign travel will make your heart sing with happiness. Plan your adventure with care. Consider some unusual locations so that you experience culture and diversity.

A home-based business that starts as a wacky idea when chatting to friends, could reap many rewards. It may not make you a millionaire but it certainly will provide you with a very comfortable lifestyle.

A surprising gift of a piece of jewellery is coming your way. This will really prove to you, just how much someone thinks of you. Accept this gracefully and wear it with pride.

666 Your 15 minutes of fame is coming. Your hard work is paying off, whether it's a TV appearance, being featured in the media or being recognised by winning a prestigious award, know that it's well deserved. Time to get the bubbly out!

667 This is a good time to change your environment in your living or office space. Redecorate, spring clean and change the furniture. Add colour and style with pictures, ornaments and soft furnishings. This will make you feel more relaxed and happy.

668 By tightening your belt through times of financial hardship can make a huge difference to your income. Switch your energy supplier, turn off lights and phone chargers when not in use. Search the internet for money saving vouchers and even start baking cakes and biscuits instead of buying them. To get extra cash quickly, collect items that you no longer need and sell them online or do a car boot sale. You could even consider renting out your car or driveway.

669 By joining your local library, you will have use of all their services including computers, photocopying and printing. You will also have access to thousands of books. Expand your knowledge by reading and join in with some of their free courses and workshops. You never know who you will meet.

670 The answer you are looking for is 'No'. This is not the right time for you to move in this direction. It's a good time to have a complete rethink about your priorities and with a little bit of courage and some support, you can change your negative situation into a healthy and positive one.

671 A surprising gift is coming your way, accept it gratefully as it is given with the very best of intentions and from a loving heart. Be grateful and thankful that someone wants to assist you. If you let pride get the better of you, your circumstances will remain the same.

 672 You don't have to be good at something to experience it. How many times have you rejected an idea or opportunity to participate in an event or activity just because you thought you would be no good at it? Come out of your comfort zone and try something new without hesitation.

 673 An upcoming birthday celebration brings people together. Remember, it doesn't have to be a big, extravagant party or an expensive meal. What is important is to spend time together. Enjoy the experience of talking about memories and sharing stories. Invite those closest to you and appreciate your family and friends.

 674 Break free from your conventional behaviours for a while. You do not have to cook a roast dinner on a Sunday or do washing on a Wednesday etc. This will relieve the pressure that you put upon yourself and give you more time to meet with friends or enjoy some long lost hobbies.

 675 A set-back makes you feel angry and annoyed. To resolve this, tackle the problem head on. There will be paperwork involved, which you will find tiresome and frustrating. If you stay calm and focussed, everything will be resolved in your favour.

676 Even when the parasite has left, the host may still itch! The time for reflection is over - the past is the past. You cannot change it. We all make mistakes and no one is perfect. Start planning for your future now. Be and feel optimistic because when the 6th June comes around, your life will be better than you expected.

677 The dilemma you're facing is certainly a challenge and something that requires expert help. Swallow your pride and approach the professionals, there really is nothing to fear. By doing this, you'll find the solution and your vitality will be restored.

678 Being spontaneous means letting go of some of the plans in your agenda. You are at risk of missing out on many exciting opportunities by being rigid and sticking to the rota too carefully. A forthcoming invitation in the next few days will test this theory. Remember, it's fun to say 'yes'.

679 Remembering our loved ones who have crossed over to the world of spirit can make us feel a huge mix of emotions. These include happiness, sadness, loneliness, grief, loss and even guilt at times. A loved one is around you right now and as their anniversary approaches, feel the love and warmth they send you.

680 You have an outgoing and friendly nature. Harness these attributes alongside your social skills and the new job that you dared to dream of will be yours by the end of the year.

681 Next Saturday's plans may well backfire and cause conflict between yourself and a friend or family member. Take a deep breath and speak your mind in a calm and diplomatic manner.

682 The 23rd April is an excellent day for matters concerning money, business and property. You can expect to be rewarded for your hard work and dedication during the last two months.

683 When organising a corporate work event or planning a day out with colleagues, make sure you check every detail thoroughly. Failure to do this will leave yourself wide open to criticism and ridicule.

684 The last few weeks have been extremely stressful for you and your family. In 14 days time, you will reach a turning point and receive information from an unexpected source which will solve a tricky problem.

685 You have great inner strength and coping mechanisms that kick in when dealing with any misfortunes that come your way. Draw upon these skills when dealing with a close friend who is going through a difficult time.

686 Your perfectionist attitude towards work and home is putting you under unrealistic pressure. Remember, you do not have to strike a ten every time you do something. It's perfectly acceptable to take time off to relax and recharge your batteries.

687 Someone around you is undertaking fertility treatment at present. This will require you to be very understanding and patient. Support is needed from professionals, friends and family, but keep your hopes up as there is luck around this situation.

688 In 3 months time your bank balance will look extremely healthy. Bright ideas will lead to success so follow your intuition.

689 A meeting with an old friend will lift your spirits and provide you with some useful information that could change the way you think about a current problem, therefore offering the solution.

690 A new pack of oracle or tarot cards will bring valuable insight into a tricky decision that you're contemplating. Trust the messages you receive as they hold the answers to your dilemma.

A legal situation is coming your way. Do plenty of research of the correct procedure you need to follow for a favourable outcome.

 Work tribunal hearings are a tricky and legal procedure. Think carefully before you go down this route. This could lead to stress and heartache. Finding a solution before things get that far is far more favourable.

 Your self-confidence is about to return and this will bring new opportunities towards you. You are capable of conquering your fears and speaking up for yourself.

 Stop being gullible and allowing someone to con you out of money. Your head is being filled with all the things you have wanted to hear for a long time but beware as there is deception around you.

 If you are trying to make a case against somebody remember, you need evidence, so keep a diary and make records of everything that has taken place.

696 By using a mediation service or having someone act as a mediator between yourself and another, will allow you to reach an amicable conclusion quickly and economically.

 697 Health concerns are a current issue for you. Your diet is playing an important role in this. It's time to enlist on a healthy one.

 698 Trust your instincts about the new person who enters your life in the next 7 days. They may offer you the world and appear to be the answer to your problems but they are not as they seem to be.

 699 Caution is required when using any power tools, lawn mowers or doing DIY for the next 10 days. Only do these jobs when you are concentrating fully, as distractions can lead to mishaps.

 700 A phase of luck and magic is around you for the next 8 weeks. Financial gain will come to you in the form of competition wins, promotions at work or by just being in the right place at the right time.

701 A new venture gets the green light and it's full steam ahead. You'll be tempted to work long hours but remember, in order to keep up the fast pace, you need plenty of sleep and wholesome food.

702 A rise in status will give your confidence a real boost, but don't let this go to your head and inflate your ego. Remember your roots and stay grounded.

703 A celebration is in order to mark the occasion of good news that'll be arriving through the post or via a telephone call. Enjoy this happy time.

704 People born under the Scorpio sign often have unconventional ideas and are attracted to alternative clothing. Reach out to the Scorpio person in your life as they need support and understanding right now.

705 A project that seems a huge undertaking is causing you anxiety and confusion over where to start. Do not panic, you haven't bitten off more than you can chew, you just need to be organised and to break the task down into bite-size pieces.

706 Due to your highly sensitive nature, you don't always conform to rules and regulations. This could lead you to receiving a fine or a rap on the knuckles by someone in authority. So, be mindful about your actions in the next few days.

707 When choosing a new vehicle, be open minded about the make and model as this could save you a lot of money in the long term. You're attracted to the colour blue, so make that one of your preferences as you embark on your search.

708 By joining a club that is sport orientated, you'll make new friends and are extremely likely to find a new love match.

709 Do not see your personal relationships as a power struggle or competition, as this will always lead to distrust and confrontation. Instead, remember why you chose to be with this person and decide whether you wish to live in harmony with them, or whether it's time to break away.

710 Whether it's you, or someone close to you, that's considering or going through a divorce right now, make sure you have all the financial documentation that's required. This includes bank statements, pension information, mortgage accounts etc.

711 Expect the 'unexpected'. Do not make any plans that you're not prepared to break. Travel is not favoured right now, postpone any arrangements for the next 21 days.

 712 A child's over-reaction to a simple problem needs further investigation. It's a sign that something in their life is troubling them.

 713 It's far better to tell the truth in this situation, instead of weaving a web of lies that will ultimately trip you up.

 714 Do not cut corners to save a few pounds where insurance and safety are concerned. Be vigilant with household and car security. Check all insurance policies are up-to-date.

 715 By enlisting on a training course linked to working in the service industry, you're securing a satisfying role for yourself in the future.

716 Drink plenty of filtered or natural spring water for the next 28 days. This will give you more energy and flush out toxins from your body.

717 A lady who passed into the spirit world draws close to you right now. You have been thinking about her and wondering how she would perceive your current situation. Know that you have her blessing.

718 Someone who's a real 'grafter' and works in the construction industry will be coming in to your life very soon. They'll be headstrong, full of fun and very loving. Give them a chance, they can make you happy.

719 Today is the day to face up to challenges and tackle them head on. Any scheduled meetings should be handled in an assertive, yet calm manner.

720 You feel as though the rug has been pulled from under your feet and circumstances are against you, but don't panic. Trust that things are changing for the better. The Universe has a plan for you and in 12 months time, life will be better than you ever hoped it would be.

721 When life throws you lemons 'make lemonade!' This is a trying and stressful time for you, but this negative situation will turn into a positive one. You'll find it difficult to think clearly at present, but know that the answers you seek are coming in an unexpected way.

722 Only share your ideas and thoughts at present with those who you completely trust. Failing to do so will see someone using this information against you.

723 Be very aware of your pet's feelings at this time. Are they behaving out of character, or acting strangely? If you are concerned, arrange for a vet check-up. This is also a time where a new pet may come into your life.

724 Work or creative projects that you have been contemplating are a real winner. Dedicate your time and energy to see this through to completion.

725 Feelings of concern, worry and at times, despair, fill your mind with negative thoughts. Expect a miracle and keep the faith, as a well-deserved opportunity will be presented to you very soon.

726 A pleasant financial surprise is on its way. Spend this money wisely as it can be invested into a new business project or to boost an existing one.

 727 Networking and socialising within your local community will form the basis of new business plans. This is a ripe time for you to build new friendships and partnerships.

 728 Try to avoid working yourself up into a state of anxiety over the next two weeks. Although problems will occur, and there will be setbacks, things will quickly resolve themselves and everything will turn out well.

 729 It's time to face your fears and stop allowing them to hold you back. Fears that are deep-rooted may need specialist help. Do some research into Cognitive Behaviour Therapy and counselling, as this could bring effective results.

 730 The name of Margaret or Mary is significant now or in the future. Take some time out of your day to practise 'mindfulness' and start to de-stress. Good news is coming around the date of 8th December.

731 By planting bulbs and flowers or growing vegetables enables you to become more grounded and stable. Eating fresh fruit will bring your body back into balance and coupled with regular exercise, you'll feel re-energised and more able to cope with life's challenges.

 732 You will find numerous useful items whilst rummaging around in boxes, drawers and cupboards, so invest some time in having a thorough re-organisation of your home.

 733 Your CV needs an overhaul! Update your skills, qualifications and experience. Due to your modest attitude, enlist the help of a trusted friend who can advise you on your best qualities to include.

 734 An act of kindness will bring great benefits to you later this year. Donate your time or some money to charity and remember what goes around comes around.

 735 Interfering with another person's plans will cause squabbles and annoyance. Allow them to approach you first before offering your services next time.

736 Physical problems can be eased by participating in appropriate exercise. Having alternative treatments such as Aromatherapy, Reiki healing, Bowen Therapy or even Acupuncture can start to relax you and give you an understand of why your body is out of balance.

737 Quizzes, competitions, bingo or any type of competitive sports etc., sees you winning big. You are entering an extremely 'lucky' phase of your life. This will last for the next 12 months so make the most of it.

738 Haggling over important purchases before you seal the deal will save you hundreds of pounds. Do not be afraid to make an offer instead of paying the full asking price.

739 It's okay to quit when something is not working out as you intended. It's best to throw in the towel and move on to something new. Do not see this as a failure, just a lesson that you were meant to learn.

740 A connection to Europe, whether it's for work or pleasure, is about to throw up an interesting challenge. Do consider this seriously, as it has the potential to bring in serious cash.

741 If you have ever wanted to open your own shop or retail outlet, then take some professional business advice. The 12th of July is the perfect time to make this dream venture happen.

742 An elderly relative or family friend needs extra assistance. Take some time to chat to them about any health issues and how they are feeling at present. It would be useful to take this information to a family meeting where some decisions can be made.

743 By attending a live music concert, you will experience fun, laughter and a link to the past. Choose the genre of music that appeals to you the most, take a friend along and let your hair down. You never know who you'll meet.

744 A male that passed over to the spirit world is sending you signs to let you know that you are loved and supported. These will be shown to you in the form of pennies in unusual places, a visit from a robin and white feathers.

745 Being a good parent can be tough at times. Show your authority by laying down ground rules and sticking to them.

746 Bury the hatchet with someone who has annoyed you. This way, you're seen by others to be the bigger person. This will place you in a position of power and will work in your favour, especially in the month of June.

747 Take extra care to wear the appropriate safety gear when participating in any sporting activity, as you're prone to sprains and injuries at present.

748 Think seriously about your career. Is it what you desire? Or are you in this profession because it's what your parents wanted for you? Do you feel it's your duty to do this work? Remember, it's your life and it's okay to say no. By changing your job or studying for something you've dreamed of doing, you're honouring your soul.

749 Be willing to forgive, especially the person who has hurt you the most. This doesn't mean you must condone their behaviour or to agree with their actions, but it's time to let go and be done with it.

750 Comparing yourself to others makes you realise that you could do a better job yourself. It's time to stop meandering around. Take action and go grab centre stage.

Being reliable, decent and honest are all credible personality traits you ought to consider in a potential partner. Being attracted to 'bad boys' or 'loose women' may give you a temporary thrill, but not long-lasting love and commitment.

Be extremely cautious when entering into any contracts or financial agreements. Double check terms and contracts, as things are not as they appear.

A chance meeting whilst out shopping will reunite you with an old friend. Make sure you swap numbers as there will be many reasons to stay in touch.

It's time to face financial difficulties head on. The way forward is to liaise with anyone you owe money to. Explain your circumstances to reach an agreement. Do not fear this action as it's a step forward in becoming debt free.

To get onto the housing ladder may seem a daunting task. There is a way for you to own your own home. Research mortgage providers and stay optimistic, as from next January the house of your dreams will be yours.

756 March 2nd sees you taking a break and booking into a luxury hotel. Appreciate and make the most of this, as it will be sometime until you can do this again.

757 A link to Ireland around September 5th will be fun and exciting for you and your family. By taking the advice from the male with the Irish accent will open many new doors for you.

758 An annoying neighbour thinks they have got the better of you. In this situation, give as good as you get and assert yourself. The person in question will then step down.

759 By making your own short films about what you are passionate about, gains you new followers and friends. Use social media to share these videos as this will boost your profile and embellish your CV.

760 Things may feel like a struggle or that you're never going to reach the conclusion on a project. Trust that the end is in sight and it will all be worth it. Christmas will be better than ever this year.

You've been hiding away for far too long. It's time to come out of the dark and show the world who you are. A new position awaits you, one that will bring fame and fortune.

You have been hurt very badly by someone who betrayed your trust. Being lied to and deceived has left you wanting to withdraw from relationships. Focus on your skills, interact with new people and a new trustworthy friend will walk into your life.

Issues around your home have been filling your head with worries and doubts. It's time to have a frank discussion with who this concerns in view to getting things straightened out. A father figure will give impartial advice.

January brings in new energy and sees you gaining closure on a past issue. This is also the perfect time for you to move forward, indulging yourself in your creative talents and pursuits, using pure essential oils will help you relax and aid restful sleep.

The reason things feel as though they're against you is because you are trying too hard to control everything. By getting regular exercise, such as walking, you'll find that the serotonin levels (feel good chemicals) in your brain will increase and in turn elevate your thoughts and bring the answers you have been searching for.

766 In your heart, you already know the answer to the questions that has been bothering you. Do what you feel is right and things will work out. All you need at this time, is some reassurance that you are on the right track.

 767 When choosing new furniture, or upgrading your home, don't be afraid to haggle or search online for local bargains. This way you'll get what you want and make huge savings.

 768 In order to achieve your dreams and to propel yourself forward in the next 2 months, you need to stop being so modest! Unless you sell yourself and point out all your amazing qualities, you risk losing out on an opportunity that will set your heart racing.

 769 Bumping into someone at the local supermarket will lead to a job offer or the chance of extra work. Make sure you have a pen and paper handy so you can give them your details for future reference.

 770 This is a magical time for you and your family. There will be new people coming in who will bring great joy to your lives. Plan and prepare birthday parties and get-togethers for extra sparkly fun!

771 Do not let a recent setback cloud your judgement when dealing with your plans for the future. You may feel as though you've been kicked in the teeth by someone you trusted, nevertheless you can do well by yourself.

772 Birds make wonderful pets! So, if you are short of space and looking for a companion, consider a budgie, parrot or even love-birds etc. They have a lot of love to share.

773 Travel plans may be disrupted so check ahead before embarking on your journey. Study the map and estimated time of arrival and make allowances for potential hold ups and delays.

774 If you're finding yourself in-between jobs then consider a post as a sales rep. Although this may seem unappealing, it will certainly tide you over and you will enjoy the social side of this role.

775 A day at the races is an invitation too good to miss. Whether this is with a group of friends or with a loved one, a fun day will be had by all.

776 Stan or Stanley is a name to remember. The 6th July sees you entering into a new phase of your life. You have been hoping for change for the last 6 months and it's now here. Do not fear this, embrace it instead.

777 A magical time awaits. Life starts to improve significantly once you accept that you can't turn the clock back. In the next 3 months, you'll find yourself in the right place at the right time. Many synchronistic events will occur during this period and these events will change your future for the better.

778 When feeling stuck, confused or in a dilemma, call upon your angels to help you. Angels are all around us but require you to invite them in before they assist. Watch your life change and heal as you invoke in this practice.

779 It takes a well-balanced and forgiving person to admit they are wrong and apologise. Step up to the mark right now and offer the hand of friendship. It's time to let bygones be bygones.

780 It may be tempting to take out a loan or to ramp up your credit card during a time of financial difficulty, but before you do, explore other alternatives first, including speaking to a debt counsellor or the Citizen's Advice Bureau. They are brilliant at what they do and will even make phone calls and set up repayment plans on your behalf.

A gift of a piece of jewellery will mean so much to the recipient. It doesn't have to be expensive as it will have plenty of sentimental value.

 A creative pursuit can calm your agitated mind and be a source of stress relief. Paint, take photographs or even make jewellery. This new hobby may even be a potential business in the future.

 It's important to spend time with young children, whether they are relatives or by working with them. You have a natural bond with children and you are able to gain their trust and boost their confidence. This activity will also be beneficial to you, as it will keep you busy and make you feel appreciated.

 Someone who has passed away to the spirit world is helping you with your current situation. This person served in the army or had a military background. They send you their love and act as your guardian angel.

 When designing a new business card or website, think carefully about your logo. Do not rush this process as this could make or break your business. This logo needs to encapsulate the essence of your brand. By including a photo of yourself, it'll make people remember you and the good service you provide.

786 Be extremely honest when dealing with legal matters or you will be caught out in the end. Do not hold back information or make any false disclosures.

 787 Helping to fund-raise or by organising an event for an animal or wildlife rescue centre will increase awareness for this cause. Enlist the help of friends or family for practical help and to brainstorm ideas.

 788 It's easy to indulge in retail therapy for a temporary fix when we are feeling worried or distracted. Remember, this can leave you with extra bills to pay so try shopping in the charity shops instead.

 789 Either you or a loved one is suffering from a fear or a phobia. For this to be helped or cured, seek the help of a qualified Hypnotherapist or Cognitive Behavioural Therapist.

 790 An object that you thought was lost and gone forever is about to turn up. This item has sentimental value to you. It'll turn up when you are sorting out your home, and when you least expect it.

791 It's time for you to join in and to meet new people. This may feel like it's a hard task for you to undertake, but in order to make new acquaintances swallow your shyness and take the plunge by seeking out like-minded people.

792 Teenagers can be hard work, challenging and often misunderstood. Take time to spend quality and meaningful time with one that's close to you. Listen to them without judgement. Ask questions about their life and what problems they are dealing with. They need your support and guidance.

793 It's time to get sporty! Go swimming, ride a bike or join a club or gym. Getting back into shape will not only make you feel physically fit and look great, it will also lift your mood, alleviate anxiety and improve your mental health.

794 The reason that the person around you is causing trouble and meddling in your life is because they are envious of your situation. Jealousy can bring out the worst in people and makes them revengeful and spiteful. Put a stop to this completely by ignoring them and blocking them out of your life.

795 When looking to relocate or getting a valuation on your property, you'll find the name of someone called 'Tina' extremely helpful. Listen to her advice, as it will help you with your decision-making process.

796 By getting your hands dirty in the garden or assisting someone in their garden or allotment, you'll find great satisfaction in creating a tranquil and productive space. It's a joy to see plants or vegetables that you've planted, watered and nurtured, grow and bloom.

 797 There's lots of DIY to do and complete. The reason that it's taking so long to finish is because you are over faced with the extent of the work. Therefore, extra help is required. Even if you have to pay a tradesman to complete the job, it'll be money well spent.

 798 If you're dreaming of an adventure abroad, then this is the optimum time to start planning it. Discuss with friends and family and others that have done a similar trip. You'll need to start saving now in order to fulfil your requirements, but it'll be an awesome vacation.

 799 Stop playing petty emotional games with your partner or friend. If this continues it will split the two of you up. Ask yourself, is this what you really want? The other person is at the end of their tether with you, so you are skating on thin ice.

 800 Congratulations! Your hard work and dedication is now starting to pay off. Things are now coming together nicely and all your planning and vision is about to materialise. The month of March will hold much fun and excitement with an incredible opportunity on offer.

Have you ever considered a job or business that involves using your culinary skills? Remember, working in the catering industry can earn you large profits. Consider how you can turn this into a lucrative business idea.

801

You have a distorted view of the situation you're asking about. This is because you're emotionally involved and therefore unable to see things as they really are. By discussing this with an outsider, you'll gain a clearer picture of what to do next.

802

A meeting at the bank will work in your favour. The 12th of next month is the perfect time to get your financial affairs in order.

803

Try not to panic, you're able to deal with this problem far easier than you realise. Do not avoid the person that has put you into this position, tackle them head on instead.

804

You career is about to go through a very busy time. Keep your diary up to date, or you will become double-booked and this will not go down well with your clients.

805

806 To create a healthier financial future, start to save now. Even if it's putting a few pounds away in a jar once a week. It'll soon add up and will enable you to make a sound investment later in the year.

 807 You're perceived as the 'rock' of the family that everyone depends on. You'll receive a request that is hard to say 'no' to. Think carefully before agreeing to this, as the consequences may outweigh any benefits.

 808 It's time to dig out and check any premium bonds, investments or savings accounts that you may have forgotten about. There's surprise money coming your way and it's just at the time when you need it the most.

 809 It's time to cut any losses and move on. A fresh plan will emerge. Just stay open-minded and flexible and the rest will follow. In 4 weeks' time, an opportunity arises.

 810 Do not be taken in by someone else's sob story. They are trying to take advantage of your good nature. You are always ready to offer a helping hand, but this time proceed with caution.

811 You have some unique abilities and it's your time to shine. Think about where your talents can lead you and how you can make the most of them. By discussing and brainstorming your ideas with a friend, it'll help turn them into reality.

 812 It's time to set some goals to work towards. With your enterprising ideas and using your intuition, your goals will be achievable and easy to attain.

 813 Beware of the male who appears to be charming and affluent. He is wearing a false mask around you and he has his own agenda for wanting to get to know you.

 814 Because of your busy lifestyle, some of your friends and family are feeling a little neglected. Let them know how much you love and appreciate them. Spend some time on a one-to-one basis. This will make a huge difference to how they feel.

 815 Doubt is your worst enemy now. Not only are you doubting yourself but you are doubting those around you. Stop fearing the worst scenario and being suspicious of others' motives. By 27th of this month, your doubts will fade as a surprising request will make you realise that you're respected and thought of highly.

816 Someone will offer the apology that you've been waiting for and will back down on a moral issue. Accept the apology gracefully and do not throw it back in their face, even though you may be tempted.

817 When you look back on some of your relationships, you realise that they've been so turbulent that they could have been made into a movie. Learn from these experiences so that you don't make the same mistakes again.

818 An upcoming anniversary around Christmas time will make you feel sad with a sense of grief. What you need to think about, is what advice that person would give you right now. By contemplating on that, your question will be answered and the way forward will become crystal clear.

819 By keeping the faith and knowing everything will be okay, will keep your spirits up. Draw upon your inner strength and be the courageous person that you are. Your life is going through a period of readjustment and it will lead to an exciting and happy future.

820 In the next 6 weeks, you will find yourself sealing a deal with an influential person. Make sure you stick to your promises where this is concerned, so that you are not being scrutinised later on.

Few are unable to resist your charms over the next few weeks! So, use this to your advantage and use this opportunity to power forwards in your work life and with your personal relationships. But remember to use this in the most purposeful of ways.

An announcement or a new addition to the family brings excitement and allows you to grow close to someone you've not seen for some time. March 28th will become a significant date in your diary and don't be surprised if travel sees you stepping onto French soil.

Consider booking a track day driving experience for that person who is difficult to buy a present for. It's something that they have been longing to do for some time. It'll show them how much you care.

Problems in your love life are easily solved, so don't give up trying. Use a little bit of spontaneity and organise a surprise trip or visit to the theatre, then your romance will be rekindled.

To lift your spirits book yourself in for a makeover, a new hairstyle and buy a sassy outfit. Take plenty of selfies and expect loads of attention. Plenty of compliments will follow and your self-confidence will be restored.

826 Speak out and put your own views across in the workplace. It's the right time to make contributions and get yourself noticed. Remember to be tactful when doing this and then when a new offer is put to you, be ready to accept.

 827 The rumours that you've heard about a friend or colleague recently are malicious gossip. Trust your instincts and be ready to defend this person. They will be overwhelmed by your loyalty and appreciate your advice over this matter.

 828 The 5th of May is a good time to sign a contract. This will be a life changing moment for you. From this date, you'll feel as though you are in a whirlwind. For the next 6 months, you will lay down foundations for your future. It will be a beneficial and productive period of hard work and negotiation.

 829 Cosy candlelit dinners, weekend breaks and being spoilt rotten are on the cards for you this summer. It'll be a refreshing change to be treated in this way. Remember, you deserve it.

 830 A friend is about to trust you with a secret that puts you into a moral dilemma. Think carefully before you break their confidence as you stand to lose their friendship. Ask yourself how much you value their friendship and are you willing to jeopardise it in order to stick to your principles?

831 You need greater emotional security from your partner. For this relationship to progress, you have need to ask some soul-searching questions. 'Do you really love them?', and 'do you trust them?' Consider whether you are in this relationship for the right reasons; 'do you fear being single?' If you're in doubt over the answers, then consider breaking free.

832 You seem to have forgotten that life is meant to be fun! Don't allow yourself to become a victim even though it would be easier at times to slip into this pattern. It's time for you to face old wounds so that healing can take place.

833 You are thinking too much about money and your finances and all this is doing is exacerbating the problem. Look at ways to cut your expenditure e.g. making a packed lunch for work, cutting out coupons, and washing the car yourself. These small changes will add up and make a difference.

834 You have some ingrained thought patterns which you have learnt from your parents. These are holding you back in your work life and relationships. Challenge these thoughts by thinking 'I am good enough to reach my highest goals and I am loveable and deserve a wonderful partner'.

835 Yourself or someone close to you is going to appear on TV in a documentary, on the news or in a magazine style programme. Make sure that you record this so that it can be shown to family and friends.

836 We all make mistakes, it's part of being human especially when we're in a bad place and feeling vulnerable. Regrets are hard to forget but don't define yourself by them. Accept you made an error of judgement and move on.

837 Encourage your partner to open up and discuss what it is that is troubling them. This may be a matter that can be assisted by making an appointment with Relate or helped by counselling sessions. Your support will be vital during this time.

838 It's time to become involved in events and activities in your local area. Your caring and sensitive nature can lend itself to giving advice and friendship to others. Research what's available by looking through adverts in newspapers, notices in shop windows and library notice boards.

839 Your imagination is running away with you over a situation that involves your partner. Listen to their side of the story and what explanation they have to offer, before making any further decisions.

840 New learning opportunities are all around you. By studying an area of complimentary therapy, you'll gain a greater understanding of restoring physical health. Therapies such as Homeopathy would be particularly beneficial for this.

841 By holding on to your old belief systems you're blocking new, stimulating and fun opportunities. You keep asking yourself 'why don't things change for me?' This is the reason why. It's time to drop your guard and live a little.

842 Just because some of your friends share similar interests and hobbies to you, doesn't automatically mean that you are on the same wavelength. Draw closer to people that you feel comfortable around, that don't put you under pressure or expect anything in return.

843 You're creating stressful situations in your life by worrying what other people think of you. Stop seeking approval from others and stop judging yourself by their opinions. It's okay to make mistakes. Let people see the real you. You're perfect just the way you are.

844 Stop doing the things you don't want to do just because you feel it's your duty to do them. It's making you feel resentful and bitter. Instead stop seeking approval from others and start to value yourself. During the next 7 weeks, focus on doing some things spontaneously without asking permission from others. This will give you freedom and a chance to reconnect with who you really are.

845 You're going to receive some flattering compliments in the next few days. Instead of brushing them off like you normally do, acknowledge the reasons why you have earned them. It's time to believe in your ambitions and to push yourself into the limelight.

846 Instead of complaining about the lack of money in your life, make a conscious effort to turn this situation around. Start by taking items back to shops, that you bought on impulse. Return faulty items that are still within the guarantee. Refunds, credit notes and even money-off vouchers will make a difference.

 847 You're feeling restless with nervous energy. In the next 4 weeks, look at improving your technical skills either with an online course, or by asking a knowledgeable friend or family member. You can learn lots by watching informative YouTube videos. By putting your new skills and restless energy together, you can launch a productive project.

 848 Friends or family who live overseas will be in touch soon, with good news and an exciting proposition. Do not instantly dismiss this, instead give it serious thought and consideration.

 849 There are teething troubles around a new venture which will make you feel disheartened and disappointed. Pick yourself up and brush yourself off, as the venture is worth pursuing.

 850 Your romantic life is about to take a turn for the better. Put aside any doubts or insecurities and enjoy the passionate time that lies ahead.

Listen to your own intuition around work, money and business. It's time to branch out into pastures new. Remember to ignore the advice from a so-called friend about this as they are putting their needs before your own.

 You are trying to lead a champagne lifestyle on a lemonade budget. Stop trying to keep up with the friends who have expensive taste. Instead, focus on your own individuality and lifestyle. Stay grounded and true to yourself and do not let your ego get the better of you.

 You are about to be rewarded in an unexpected way. Something you have been day dreaming about is about to turn into a reality. The next 6 months will be full of fun and adventure.

 Your diary is about to become full of enjoyable social invitations. Make sure your wardrobe has a few glamorous outfits to suit each occasion as there won't be much time for shopping in the next 10 weeks!

 A meeting with a stranger at a party or social event will prove to be very beneficial. This person has an unusual job which will inspire and motivate you. It's a good idea to stay in touch with them and to meet up on a regular basis.

856 A person connected to your past will re-establish contact. They will lead you to believe that they have turned over a new leaf and have mended their ways. Go with your gut instinct and take things cautiously.

 857 You are about to book a holiday but you are unsure about the location. The best way to make this decision is to go to a destination that a trusted friend has recommended. That way you will start to relax and plan accordingly.

 858 A close family member requires some extra care and assistance. It's time to put their needs before your own. Extra help will come but this will take 2-4 weeks to organise properly so your loyalty will be required in the interim period.

 859 You're feeling frustrated and annoyed about your current working situation. Someone's been treating you in an unfair manner and even though you've made your feelings known, nothing seems to have changed. It's time to move on, even if you take a position that you feel is out of your comfort zone, it will be an improvement and will only be temporary. The 20th May sees a job prospect that's too good to turn down.

 860 At last new doors are opening for you. Your hard work is paying off which is about to lead to a better lifestyle and a future that you've been dreaming of.

861 A friendship is about to turn into romance. This may come as a surprise to you as you've been unaware of how this person feels towards you. It's good to take things slowly to begin with, but as the love between you grows, so will the passion.

862 It's worth pursuing a money-making opportunity that will be presented to you. It's a very feasible idea, it just needs to be marketed in the right way and to a captive audience.

863 Ignoring problems could lead to serious consequences so stop burying your head in the sand and tackle things head on. You'll feel so much better when you're actively dealing with them. Pleasing results will follow.

864 When poorly or feeling under the weather, it's foolish to try and rush the recovery. Allow your body and mind to rest and heal itself. Nurture yourself and allow others to assist you.

865 A nice surprise is on its way to you. It won't be what you're expecting and you may feel a little perplexed by it. Nevertheless, accept it and enjoy.

866 You're trying too hard to make things happen. Stop trying to chase your dreams, instead allow them to happen and unfold naturally.

867 It's time to make changes to your appearance. For inspiration look through magazines, books or even on the internet. Confide in a friend for advice and go shopping to try new clothes styles.

868 What service could you offer if you're thinking about going self-employed? Allow your imagination to run a little wild and see yourself succeeding. Your name will be on a business card in the next 6-8 months.

869 When out on a date, you'll make a big impression by just being you. You are kind, caring, generous and charismatic. Do not wear a false mask or worry about what perception your date has of you. Enjoy it and relax.

870 There is a lot of romantic interest around you right now. Be ready to accept compliments, invitations and to attend social functions.

871 Money that has been promised to you for some time is about to come through. Do not waste it, as you'll be tempted to blow it all in one go. Instead, spend a little of it and save the rest for a rainy day.

 872 Someone is about to plead poverty to you. Give them advice about how they can improve their situation and how to stop squandering money. Don't lend them your hard-earned cash unless you can afford to lose it.

 873 An upcoming business trip will seem like a drag but it will turn into an exciting adventure. New contacts will be made and this leads to important meetings later in the year.

 874 It's time to stop having regrets about the past, especially in the relationship department. Love is blind and you certainly got your fingers burnt and learnt the hard way. Remember though, not everyone is like that, so stop judging potential partners on your past mistakes.

 875 After picking up where you left off a few years ago, you'll be offered a transformational role. Life is good at last, and will never be the same again.

876 Take a chance on love. Stop hiding yourself away and making excuses not to see other people. A new person is coming along for you and they will transform your life for the better.

877 Searching for an old friend or ex-partner brings happy times into your future. It just takes a little courage and commitment to find who you are looking for.

878 Treating yourself to the good things in life needn't be a sin. Enjoy being wined and dined. You deserve it.

879 Draw your children close to you. Do old fashioned activities such as colouring, baking and playing board games. This will bring back happy memories and bring your bond even closer together.

880 By delivering an act of kindness, shows not only do you care, but tells the Universe you are ready to receive positivity and abundance into your life.

Visit a charity shop and buy a book. There's a book waiting for you that's going to bring motivation, and excellent information about starting your own business.

 By starting a simple daily exercise routine, even if it's just for 20 minutes, will increase your stamina, muscle tone and your energy levels.

 Look out for the name of 'Littlewood' as a surname or street/place name. This will prove to be significant information that will assist you greatly in the search for something you thought was lost.

 It's time for you to stop suppressing your own creativity and to express your vision. Whether it's designing your own t-shirts, being an interior designer, taking a course in photography or being a book illustrator etc. Whatever your passion, this is the right time to take a step forward and embrace your talents.

 You feel as though you are in limbo and things are not moving forward as fast as you like. Instead of fretting over this, use your time productively. Remember this saying, 'When fishermen are not able to go to sea, they stay at home and repair their nets instead.'

886 Everything is beginning to synchronise beautifully for you. Your thoughts and ideas are hitting the mark and your inspirations and goals are aligning. In the next 4 weeks, you'll see your dreams turn into reality.

887 By tying up loose ends, finishing off uncompleted projects and tasks that you've been putting off for some time, puts you in a position of reaching a state of psychological closure. Now you're able to wipe the slate clean and embark on new friendships and relationships.

888 You've reached a magical time in your life. It's about to be filled with beautiful people. At last your financial worries and constraints are about to be alleviated and will bring with it a new sense of freedom and upliftment. Embrace your wonderful life and live it to the full.

889 Long distance relationships can be hard to manage and will require plenty of trust and commitment. Are you truly prepared to be put in a position where you would be asked to make a choice about upping sticks and moving away from your family and friends? This will ultimately test your relationship. Think very carefully before proceeding.

890 News of an engagement is coming! This will be an exciting and exhilarating time for you and your family.

891 Beware of fakery! When purchasing goods be sure they are genuine and authentic. That goes for new people coming into your life as well. Be wary of someone's ulterior motives for the next 12 weeks.

892 People can take advantage of your good nature. When a friend asks for a favour out of the blue, be strong enough to say 'no' as this will reset the boundaries you share with them. Do not allow yourself to be used.

893 For the next 3 weeks, focus on healing your body and mind. Cut out sugar to restore and rebalance your body. Eat plenty of fruit, vegetables and don't forget to include nuts, seeds and brown rice. Make a list of your goals for the next 6 months, as you are far more likely to achieve them if you write them down. This routine will also improve your sleep pattern.

894 It's time to join forces with your loyal friends and family to allow them to support you during the next 6 weeks. This will be a time of change and opportunity for you. Ultimately this will all work out for the best but there will be a few speed bumps along the way.

895 Old feelings from a past love are set to return. Think carefully before acting on this, as you're seeing things through rose coloured glasses. This person will try and convince you that they have changed, but is this the case?

896 It's time for a dose of global culture. Go and pick up some holiday brochures and allow your mind to wander. Better still, do your own research by talking to friends about unusual holiday escapes.

897 You may be fiercely independent but you crave company right now. There will be many romantic encounters and options for you to choose from, but stay grounded and keep a level head when arranging dates.

898 It's the right time to develop your own brand, whether it's clothing, make-up or something food related. It's starred for success. Liaise with companies who can supply you and attend trade shows and seminars in order to make this happen.

899 Be bold, speak your mind without hesitation as you have kept quiet and had to bite your tongue many times over the last 6 weeks. It's time for the truth. Be courageous and act quickly.

900 The next 4 weeks is the best time to take your income to a new level. Be ambitious, make new plans and take a chance. There's no time to waste, your time to soar is now.

901 Get your diary in order and get everything up-to-date. You are in for a frenzied 30 days of work and adventure. This will see you physically and mentally exhausted, but it will be worth it and you will reap the rewards later this year.

902 You are emotionally over-loaded, therefore not seeing things clearly. Stop wasting your time on idle gossip, just say what you mean, and mean what you say.

903 Joyfulness is within easy reach. Enjoy the next 6 months and allow yourself to feel relaxed about the future. New contentment is with you, as you're about to find what you have been searching for.

904 You are a natural actor. You're talented at altering your appearance and persona. Think about joining a theatre group and having singing lessons.

905 Enjoy the process of writing. It's time to express yourself with creative writing. Start by thinking of your favourite subject or hobby and see how you can encapsulate the essence of that into a story.

906 Remember, you're a force to be reckoned with. Stand your ground and do not take no for an answer. Speak from a place of truth and integrity in order to be victorious in this situation.

907 Allow yourself to release your emotions, cry and laugh as much as you need to. This will help relieve some of the pressure that you have been under over the last 9 weeks.

908 A secret is about to unravel itself. It's better to come clean and be brutally honest when dealing with this situation, than trying to cover up the facts.

909 The rebellious side of you loves to live life on the edge and it won't be long before you receive the adrenaline rush you crave. Plan your adventure precisely and in detail.

910 Situations in which you perceive as unfortunate often turn into blessings. Focus on that analogy for the next 7 days, as this will shift your perception of the current situation.

911 From the 5th July, you're in a prime position to join the world of entertainment. Make preparation for this by updating your CV, website and profile.

912 Being extremely tactful is the best way forward in order to avoid offending a friend or loved one. Your opinion matters, but in this instance diplomacy outweighs your personal viewpoint.

913 Someone with the star sign of Leo needs your understanding and advice. Try not to interrupt them when they open up to you. Instead, listen carefully and put yourself in their shoes and see things from their perspective.

914 During the spring time, you will have a burst of new energy and your zest for life will be restored. Being around young children will make you feel valued and needed. This will bring fun and laughter into your household.

915 When choosing a holiday destination, consider Florida or Australia. Include aquatic themed attractions such as SeaWorld, swimming with dolphins, or even jet-skiing and water sports. Water and the ocean will bring excitement and adventure.

916 Repel those negative thoughts you keep having about yourself. Don't rush into a decision while you're in this frame of mind. Instead, boost your ego by socialising with loyal and trusted friends that don't criticise or put you down. Remember, you're beautiful, kind and sincere. It's time to eliminate people who do not make you feel loved and appreciated.

917 Instead of talking about someone behind their back, face up to them and tell them how you feel. Do not make a mountain out of a molehill when an unexpected setback happens later this week. Instead, reconsider a decision that you recently made, as it's time to re-assess the situation.

918 Get your finances in order. Look at switching your credit card to a 0% balance transfer, look for a cheaper energy supplier and even start baking your own cakes. Take packed lunches to work and take a flask or refillable cup on outings. These changes will save you pounds.

919 It's not about what car you own, if you have the latest tech gadgets or wear designer clothes. It's about feeling happy and contented in your life. Soul searching is required. Drop your ego and stop focussing on what other people think of you. Be the best person you can by being kind and thoughtful. Spend time with like-minded friends and if they don't think similarly, then it's time to find new ones.

920 Good news is coming and life is going to start speeding up. The next 28 days sees a resolution to an ongoing problem and will bring relief and a new sense of fun for the future months ahead.

921 From 4th May you will have the 'luck of the Irish' with you. Carry with you a lucky charm or talisman to represent this. Push yourself forward and test yourself, as you're capable of so much more.

922 Trust in your own strengths and abilities to overcome this situation. Someone with the name of 'Edge' or 'Edgeware' will give you valuable information that will assist in your success.

923 Diets may work initially, but over time the weight will creep back on so don't waste money by buying expensive diet foods or shakes. Instead, eat mindfully, and reduce your sugar intake. Have plenty of fresh fruit and vegetables, chew and savour every mouthful and sit at the table. Reduce portion size, incorporate some daily exercise and you'll see the pounds disappear.

924 You can live without your vices. You only have weak willpower if you think you do. Be honest with yourself and cut out any addictions or habits e.g., smoking, drinking, caffeine, or shopping etc. You can do it. Just imagine how much better you'll feel, and how much more money you'll have. What an achievement!

925 Only take on a loan if you're certain you can pay it back. Borrowing money off friends or family can be the quickest way to fall out and create arguments and pressure.

926 Your partner will need support and encouragement as they move from one job to another. This will increase their earning potential. There will be longer hours and new training to start with but it will prove to be a rewarding and fulfilling role.

927 Do not put up with an unfair and unjust situation just because you don't want to face conflict. This scenario needs to be faced and worked through for the good of everyone involved.

928 You are feeling confused and need guidance as you try to make this decision. Ask the Universe to send you a sign. Even if you are sceptical, do it anyway. Then become very aware of your environment. The sign will come, usually very quickly. Look out for messages on billboards, shop windows and even on buses etc. The answer will be shown to you.

929 Instead of moaning about your home environment, de-clutter it and change it. Gift some of the things you no longer need to a friend or family member who'll appreciate it. Recycle your tired furniture by painting it with a colour you love. You can even make simple cushions, toys, and patchwork throws from your old clothes.

930 A chance meeting on 20th of the month leads to new opportunities. This person will be connected to the events industry or works in the media. You'll have a lot in common and plenty to discuss.

931 Remember relationships and partnerships are all about compromise. Therefore, you have a big decision to make. Are you able to make the required compromises in order to stay in this partnership? If not, now is the time to cut loose.

932 You are being far too stubborn in your attitude and this is causing friction between you and a loved one. It takes the bigger person to 'back down' and admit they are in the wrong. If you refuse to do this, then you will suffer the consequences.

933 Home is your sanctuary, the place where you feel safe and secure. It's a good time to enhance your home by redecorating, revamping old furniture and even reconfiguring your living space.

934 Life is becoming more complicated than it needs to be. A lot of these complications can easily be resolved by making a 'plan of action'. Make phone calls to explain your current situation as this will resolve many problems.

935 Inabilities to make decisions will cause you problems. When you feel indecisive, talk things through with a good friend and listen to their advice. This will prove to be one of the best decisions that you will make. It will give you head space and allow you to see things clearly at last.

936 You can utilise your logical, common-sense outlook into business coaching. You're capable of making sound business plans and even see the potential in others when they have lost their way. Financial success will come from good judgement and by trusting your gut instinct.

 937 Due to your loyal nature and your ability to keep secrets, you are suited to confidential lines of work. This will also require you to be non-judgemental and a good listener. Some of these situations my be of a sensitive or serious nature so think before you speak.

 938 You have some hidden treasures within your home. By getting items valued, you will be pleasantly surprised. Do not hold onto them for sentimental reasons when you could benefit greatly from the money they can bring.

 939 A dinner date invitation is coming your way within the next 4 weeks. Accept it, dress up and go out in style. It's time to have fun and throw caution to the wind.

 940 You will be required to do some public speaking. There's no need to fear this, as once you start your speech, there will be no stopping you. You will actually enjoy the experience and opportunity of speaking about a subject that is close to your heart.

Physical health improvements see you brimming with energy and vitality. This significantly improves your confidence and you'll develop a new interest in clothes, facial skincare and looking good. Plenty of compliments will follow but this may make others feel jealous and insecure, so be mindful and diplomatic about how your new transformation could affect others. Reassure them that your feelings for them are as strong as ever.

Mistakes and mix-ups associated with paperwork can cause problems for you. Be vigilant when filling in forms, tax returns and other important documents. When an inaccuracy or delay shows up, communicate with those involved quickly to rectify any mishaps.

A new love affair brings excitement and romance into your life. Common sense will not be on your radar as you become swept along with the intensity of this relationship. Remember, it's okay for you to feel like this and you can deal with all the practicalities later.

Someone close to you is about to sign divorce papers. They're putting on a brave face. The last few months has caused them stress and anguish. Be supportive and understanding and include them in any outings and events you have planned. There is plenty of life for them after their divorce. In six months' time, a dramatic change of events sees them happier than ever.

It's time to make travel plans to explore and discover areas of the world which you've always dreamed of visiting. A lucky windfall will enable this.

946 There are twins coming into your life so look out for a new friend who has a twin brother or sister or even the birth of twin babies. If you already have twins in your family or friendship circle, then it's time to offer them your support.

 947 The end of a long career is approaching fast. This may leave you feeling anxious and sad but it paves the way for a new and exhilarating job offer.

 948 You will be giving a performance that will open new doors for you. When you see your name in print, your heart will feel full of pride but also anticipation. The spotlight is on you, so make the most of it.

 949 Recognition for the work you've already done will come in a surprising way. You're about to be head hunted. This will leave you in a dilemma about whether to accept an offer or not. Go for it, you have earned this opportunity.

 950 You need more action and stimulation in your life. Due to your tolerant nature, people can be misled into thinking you are happy with the way things are. This is leading you to be temperamental and discontented. Life is for living, it's time to be more adventurous.

951 Your financial position by the end of this month is looking good. Be careful not to jeopardise this by excessive spending or splashing the cash when out with friends. Be realistic and do not be tempted to spend more than you can afford.

952 A friend is about to confide in you with a large juicy secret. You will feel tempted to tell others, but if you betray your friend, you will lose them forever.

953 It's important to air your opinions and speak out, especially when you want to promote a good cause. Write letters, attend local council meetings or even phone local radio stations. It's time to be heard.

954 You are about to become immersed into a new sport or exercise regime. Due to your excitement and eagerness you're at risk of pushing your body too far, too soon. Pace yourself and build up gradually and sensibly as that will ensure you keep any injuries or strains to a minimum.

955 It's time to recognise any financial commitments that are due to you. Are you receiving everything that you're entitled to? Whether it's child maintenance payments, living allowances or other benefits, you are at risk of not claiming what is rightfully yours.

956 Be careful not to allow your impulsive energy to get the better of you. You will have an overwhelming feeling to say 'yes' to just about everything for the next 14 days. Resist the temptation and instead sleep on it first before committing yourself.

957 A new acquaintance who gives you a first impression of being 'plain and boring' couldn't be further from the truth. Give yourself a chance to get to know them better, as their true self will emerge.

958 A romantic gesture is coming your way. This demonstrates how much you're loved and cared for. Stop doubting your relationship and be fully immersed in the moment.

959 Allow new friendships to develop, especially those connected to your work as they will become strong and loyal allies. In the past, you've attracted friendships that have been full of negativity. Consequently, this has made you question new people who have come into your life.

960 You cannot force anyone to change, they can only do this if they want to. If you cannot put up with the way they are, then it's time to walk away.

961 You have been anticipating change and it's about to come. This will allow you to evolve. Worries will fade and your fears will dissolve. Heaven is watching over you and your dreams are about to turn into reality.

962 A brilliant business idea is coming to you. Before you act on it, brainstorm your ideas with friends and family. This idea is starred with success, nevertheless preparation is key. Feedback from those you trust will steer you in the best direction and see your business grow from strength to strength.

963 It's time to rightfully claim what's yours. Whether it's taking back faulty goods or claiming benefits, there is financial prosperity awaiting you. Check any Premium Bonds or lottery tickets.

964 It's time to go that extra mile to help someone that you don't even know. A friend of a friend needs advice and support from you. This person requires your expertise and knowledge in order to solve a problem. There will be no financial gains for your services but your act of kindness will bring a far greater reward and enhance your reputation.

965 You've been mixed up in a situation that's underpinned by dishonesty and deceit. It's time to come clean, tell the truth and hold your head up high. This way you are giving yourself the best outcome. As you turn your back on the old, you're embracing a happy and fulfilling future with your soul mate.

966 Don't allow your fear of being judged and criticised stop you from making a stand for what you believe in. Undoubtedly you'll face disapproval from some small-minded individuals but as you take the lead, the right people will flock towards you and your cause.

967 Due to a past betrayal, trusting people around you has now become difficult and your judgement has become clouded. To combat this, think of 2 people who you trust and why. Write down what makes them so and use that blueprint to gauge characteristics in new people. You'll soon see that someone who gets close to you is genuinely loyal and kind.

968 Stress is an overwhelming factor. It's affecting your physical, emotional and spiritual sides of life. By creating a 'sacred space' in your home you'll have somewhere to go that's private, comfortable and relaxing. Use mindfulness techniques and meditation and order will start to be restored.

969 You've started to neglect your spiritual side. The simple act of walking in nature will reconnect and ground you. You'll gain a sense of proportion of what's really important. Book a holiday that includes coastal or riverside walks. If you're lucky enough to find yourself next to a natural waterfall, take a photo or video so you can evoke 'feel good memories' when you're back home.

970 It's time for your passion to be reawakened with a new partner. Use your sexual power to attract a new person into your life. Excitement, sensuality and fun times will be yours in the next 6 weeks.

Travel plans see you embracing your dreams by venturing outside your comfort zone. If you're puzzling over where to go, then consider New Zealand! You will find it offers everything on your wish list.

Seek counselling or support groups, as you've a tendency to squander money on material possessions. People with this trait are hiding behind the real truth and use it as a sticking plaster instead of getting to the root of the problem. It's time to allow your deep-rooted fears and anxieties to surface.

Something beautiful is going to grow out of a turbulent situation. As it passes and you let go of your anger, a new creative idea will come. Your artistic side is about to kick in and by reaching out to other people with similar interests, your idea will snowball and gain plenty of interest and prosperity.

You have a relationship around you that's worth fighting for. Do not be tempted to give up too easily. This person will not be impressed if you don't fight for them and let your feelings known. It's time to swallow your pride and get off your high moral standpoint and go and get what you want.

You're feeling stuck and indecisive a greater understanding of your personality is called for. By doing self-awareness exercises (many of these can be found online) you'll start to discover what makes you 'tick'. Ultimately this leads you to have a strong link to your spiritual self and your mission and purpose for the future.

976 It's time to trust your own decision-making process. The only thing stopping you, is your own fears and self-doubts. You're thinking too far ahead about different outcomes and this is what's holding you back. It's make your mind up time.

977 By not exercising 'self-acceptance' you're becoming 'self-destructive'. Have you forgotten what a kind, loving and wonderful person you are? People love the real genuine you. Let go of any fake persona's and immediately the pressure will release.

978 Writing an autobiography may sound like an ego-led exercise. You have strong lessons to share. Therefore, others will benefit and take inspiration from your story. So, by acknowledging that it's not egotistical to write about your life's experiences, you are taking the first steps to being an author.

979 You have been keeping a secret or hiding something in order to protect yourself. It's foolish to keep up this façade any longer. The way forward is to join forces with others, as after all, there is strength in numbers. By Easter you will have undertaken this challenge with positive results.

980 The inner detective in you will see you researching and putting pieces of information together. You best work will be done at night. You will be triumphant in solving this mystery although it's useful to join forces with another.

981 Create your own group either on Facebook or in your local community. The subject will be your passion, hobby or lifestyle. There are like-minded people out there who will welcome this. New friends and associates will enhance your life and restore your faith in human nature.

982 A romantic trip abroad will be suggested in the next 30 days. Amsterdam would fit the bill perfectly. It's wise for you to take on the role of the planning and organisation so that everything goes without a hitch. But allow the other person to pay, as it's their treat for you.

983 You have been hurt deeply recently by someone's harsh words and lack of understanding about your actions. The way to get your story across is to write them a letter explaining your motives and reasons. Direct confrontations are to be avoided at present.

984 When we lose someone we love dearly, we naturally enter a grieving process. This can take many forms including sadness, anger, denial and even hopelessness. There is a loved one around you, sending you loving signs from the spirit world. Look out for robins, electrical disturbances and coins in strange places as validation of their presence.

985 By 28th July new love will have found you. This person will not be your usual type and this is an extremely beneficial thing. They'll match you with their outlook on life including their material possessions and financial status. There's no hidden agenda here, just a mutual loving relationship.

986 You're more than capable of changing the way you view your life. By challenging your beliefs about yourself you can make huge, positive steps to increase your mind power. Rise from the dark place you've become lost in and start to love yourself. You're about to rediscover how amazing you are, and life becomes wonderful.

987 Yourself or someone around you needs to follow their own path in relation to IVF and having a baby. Go on a mission and your research will pay off. Age is a factor to consider but where there's a will, there's a way!

988 Following a health setback, it's time to be determined. Good things are coming and that will include a better financial outlook. The name of Sally will be involved in giving you sound business advice.

989 You are heading into a huge successful period of your life. Interviews and auditions will go better than anticipated with call backs and further interest. You are a star, be proud of yourself as you're ready to shine.

990 The next 28 days is your 'clearing' time. Get rid of the old things that you never use. Then go through your phone contacts and delete the people that you do not need or hear from. A Facebook cull is next, delete those negative so-called friends that are blocking your progress. You have now made space for new people to enrich your life.

991 Look out for someone with the name of 'Jennifer'. They hold crucial information which can really assist a project that you've struggled to get off the ground. Do not give up on this, as the miracle is about to happen.

992 By identifying the cause of your stress, you can begin to eliminate it from your life. Work is the underlying factor here so take the next steps to alter your routine and to branch out into something new. You can follow your dreams, it just takes self-belief and courage. October is the perfect time to put this into action.

993 You have an amazing and unique gift. Do not shy away from this, it's there to be shared with others. Your sensitive nature absorbs fears and criticisms easily and that's what holds you back. Push yourself into the limelight now, face your fears and you will realise that your achievements and success will counteract them.

994 You are the person today because of what you've seen, faced and experienced in the past. You have not allowed yourself to become a victim. You have guts and this has shaped you to become a natural leader for others. Embrace these skills and go after what you want.

995 You cannot control somebody, only help them. Likewise, you cannot change them, they must want to change themselves. If you're unable to accept them for who they are, then it's time to walk away. You will not only release yourself but them as well.

996 Step out of the shadows and into the light, you have been reinventing yourself by improving your education, therefore your knowledge. Your hard work is about to be rewarded. This will come about in a surprising and flattering way. You're ready to take on this new chapter of your life.

997 It can take years to find your true soul mate. You are both ready now to come together and connect. The sparks will fly, your heart will race, yet it will all feel natural and easy.

998 No more procrastination and no more excuses. You are going through a period of acceleration. Finish what you've started. This is your time of completion. Your motivation will now be restored and your thinking becomes clear.

999 Stop chasing your dreams and go and grab them instead. You're ready to spread your wings and fly. Think of yourself as a golden eagle, seeing things from a broader perspective. This is a time of great spiritual awakening, a time to manifest your goals and to exude confidence and capability. It's your time to shine.

1000 Your struggles are over, your hard work and dedication will now pay off. You're the captain of your own ship, and taking command of your own destiny. You have activated a life full of purpose and discovery. Your greatness is about to be recognised by others and with that brings respect and notoriety. Feel proud of your achievements and who you have become. Spread your love and light to those who come towards you. The world is a far greater place for you being in it.

About the Author

Psychic Medium, Animal Communicator and Reiki Master, Elizabeth Barber, aka 'Psychic Beth' is one of the most diverse Psychic Mediums working in the UK today. She views her work as a privilege and feels honoured to have helped many people and animals, by using her psychic abilities.

For five years Beth had nursed and grown her well-known radio show 'Psychic Beth's Spiritual Calling' on The Bridge Radio, a local station in the West Midlands. The show has seen many special guests, including well-known psychics, mediums and people who work in the mind, body and spirit industry, including Derek Acorah, Colin Fry, Gordon Smith, TJ Higgs, Philip Solomon, Ralph Keeton, Mike Davies, Jacky Newcomb, Jenny Smedley, Jackie Weaver, Gary Manion, Wendy Binks, Dave Williams, Lorraine Mills, Sarah May, Andrew Dee, Tori Hartman, Dr. Laurie Nadell, Delphi Ellis and many more.

She has also made several TV appearances including The Richard & Judy Show (Channel 4), Russell Brands Ponderland (Channel 4), Central News (ITV), Central Extra Documentary: Missing Pets (ITV), Trisha Goddards Animal Special (Channel 5) and more recently had interviews on 'Cuppa TV' (Made in Birmingham) 'Election Special' with Monica Price (Made in Birmingham) and 'In Bed with the Fizzogs' (Made in Birmingham)

Along with her radio and TV appearances, she's had magazine and newspaper features too, of which some include Woman's Own, Chat its Fate, Psychic News, Our Dogs, Fate and Fortune, The Daily Record, The Guardian, The Sunday Mercury and many more.

Beth's professional background has seen her working in both Primary and Higher Education, running her own retail business, and gaining numerous counselling qualifications which has given her a greater understanding of people, influencing her success as a psychic medium and development teacher.

Beth currently resides in the Spa town of Malvern with her partner Nigel, Alice her daughter, Angel the Jack Russell and Marty the African Grey Parrot. She has four children; Rachael, Kieran, Alice and stepson Matt.

If you wish to contact Beth and to see future events,
training workshops, and personal readings
visit the following website:
www.psychicbeth.com

For further information about this book please visit:
www.lifebynumbers.co.uk

www.universalnumberattraction.com

Connect with Beth on Facebook
@PsychicBeth

@Life by Numbers
@Animal Communication and Pet Psychics

Acknowledgements

Grateful thanks to my good friend Jane, for her relentless support and encouragement.

Without the support from my partner Nigel, my children Rachael, Kieran, and his girlfriend Molleigh, Alice and stepson Matt, my wonderful parents Dot and Keith, my sister Angela and brother-in-law Derek, my nieces Hannah and Sophie and the rest of my loving and loyal family, friends and clients, this book would not have been possible. Also Alexa, from The Book Refinery, who's help and support has finally got this book published.

53346953R00124

Made in the USA
Middletown, DE
30 November 2017